The Master Key To This Mystical Life Of Ours

by Ralph Waldo Trine

D1262016

Wilder Publications, LLC.
PO Box 3005
Radford VA 24143-3005

ISBN 10: 1-60459-044-0
ISBN 13: 978-1-60459-044-9

First Edition

10 9 8 7 6 5 4 3 2 1

Table of Contents

The Master Key To This Mystical Life Of Ours

The Fresh Beginning

There is a divine sequence running throughout the universe. Within and above and below the human will incessantly works the Divine will. To come into harmony with it and thereby with all the higher laws and forces, to come then into league and to work in conjunction with them, in order that they can work in league and in conjunction with us, is to come into the chain of this wonderful sequence. This is the secret of all success. This is to come into the possession of unknown riches, into the realization of undreamed-of powers.— *In Tune with the Infinite.*

When one awakes from sleep and so returns to conscious life, he is in a peculiarly receptive and impressionable state. All relations with the material world have for a time been shut off, the mind is in a freer and more natural state, resembling somewhat a sensitive plate, where impressions can readily leave their traces. This is why many times the highest and truest impressions come to one in the early morning hours, before the activities of the day and their attendant distractions have exerted an influence. This is one reason why many people can do their best work in the early hours of the day.

But this fact is also a most valuable one in connection with the moulding of everyday life. The mind is at this time as a clean sheet of paper. We can most valuably use this quiet, receptive, impressionable period by wisely directing the activities of the mind along the highest and most desirable paths, and thus, so to speak, set the pace for the day.

Each morning is a fresh beginning. We are, as it were, just beginning life. We have it entirely in our own hands. And when the morning with its fresh beginning comes, all yesterdays should be yesterdays, with which we have nothing to do. Sufficient is it to know that the way we lived our yesterday has determined for us our today. And, again, when the morning with its fresh beginning comes, all tomorrows should be tomorrows, with which we have nothing to do. Sufficient to know that the way we live our today determines our tomorrow.

"Every day is a fresh beginning, Every morn is the world made new; You who are weary of sorrow and sinning, Here is a beautiful hope for you, A hope for me and a hope for you.

"Ah the past things are past and over, The tasks are done, and the tears are shed. Yesterday's errors let yesterday cover; Yesterday's wounds, which smarted and bled, Are healed with the healing which night has shed.

"Let them go, since we cannot relieve them, Cannot undo and cannot atone. God in His mercy receive, forgive them! Only the new days are our own. Today is ours, and today alone.

"Here are the skies all burnished brightly; Here is the spent earth all reborn; Here are the tired limbs springing lightly, To face the sun and to share with the morn, In the chrism of dew and the cool of dawn.

"Every day is a fresh beginning, Listen, my soul, to the glad refrain, And, spite of old sorrow and older sinning, And puzzles forecasted, and possible pain, Take heart with the day and begin again."

Simply the first hour of this new day, with all its richness and glory, with all its sublime and eternity-determining possibilities, and each succeeding hour as it comes, but not before it comes. This is the secret of character building. This simple method will bring anyone to the realization of the highest life that can be even conceived of, and there is nothing in this connection that can be conceived of that cannot be realized somehow, some-when, somewhere.

This brings such a life within the possibilities of all, for there is no one, if really in earnest and if he really desires it, who cannot live to his highest for a single hour. But even though there should be, if he is only earnest in his endeavor, then, through the law that like builds like, he will be able to come a little nearer to it the next hour, and still nearer the next, and the next, until sooner or later comes the time when it becomes the natural, and any other would require the effort. . In this way one becomes in love and in league with the highest and best in the universe, and as a consequence, the highest and best in the universe becomes in love and in league with him. They aid him at every turn; they seem literally to move all things his way, because, forsooth, he has first moved their way.— *In Tune with the Infinite*

The Supreme Fact Of Human Life

The great central fact in human life is the coming into a conscious, vital realization of our oneness with the Infinite Life, and the opening of ourselves fully to this divine inflow. "I and the Father are one," said the Master. In this we see how He recognized His oneness with the Father's life. Again He said, "The words that I speak unto you I speak not of myself: but the Father that dwelleth in me, He doeth the works." In this we see how clearly He recognized the fact that He of Himself could do nothing, only as He worked in conjunction with the Father. Again, "My Father works and I work." In other words, my Father sends the power, I open myself to it, and work in conjunction with it.

Again He said, "Seek ye first the kingdom of God and His righteousness, and all these things shall be added unto you." And He left us not in the dark as to exactly what He meant by this, for again He said, "Say not Lo here nor lo there; know ye not that the kingdom of heaven is within you?" According to his teaching the kingdom of God and the kingdom of heaven were one and the same. If, then, His teaching is that the kingdom of heaven is in us, do we not clearly see that, putting it in other words, His injunction is nothing more nor less than, Come ye into a conscious realization of your oneness with the Father's life. As you realize this oneness you find the kingdom, and when you find this, all things else shall follow.

Again, the Master said, "Call no man your Father upon the earth: for one is your Father, which is in heaven." Here He recognized the fact that the real life is direct from the life of God. Our fathers and our mothers are the agents that give us the bodies, the houses in which we live, but the real life comes from the Infinite Source of Life, God, who is our Father.

One day word was brought to the Master that his mother and his brethren were without, wishing to speak with Him. "Who is my mother and who are my brethren?" said He. "Whosoever shall do the will of my Father which is in heaven, the same is my brother, and my sister, and mother."

Many people are greatly enslaved by what we term ties of relationship. It is well, however, for us to remember that our true relatives are not necessarily those who are connected with us by ties of blood. Our truest relatives are those who are nearest akin to us in mind, in soul, in spirit. Our nearest relatives may be those living on the opposite side of the globe, — people whom we may never have seen as yet, but to whom we will yet be drawn, either in this form of life or in another, through that ever working and never failing law of attraction.

When the Master gave the injunction, "Call no man your father upon the earth: for one is your Father, which is in heaven," He here gave us the basis for that grand conception of the fatherhood of God. And if God is equally the Father of all, then we have here the basis for the brotherhood of man. But there is, in a sense, a conception still higher than this, namely, the oneness of man and God, and hence the oneness of the whole human race. When we realize this fact, then we clearly see how in the degree that we come into the realization of our oneness with the Infinite Life, and so, every step that we make Godward, we aid in lifting all mankind up to this realization, and enable them, in turn, to make a step Godward.

The Master again pointed out our true relations with the Infinite Life when He said, "Except ye become as little children ye shall not enter into the kingdom of heaven." When He said, "Man shall not live by bread alone, but by every word that proceedeth out of the mouth of God," He gave utterance to a truth of far greater import than we have as yet commenced fully to grasp. Here He taught that even the physical life can not be maintained by material food alone, but that one's connection with this Infinite Source determines to a very great extent the condition of even the bodily structure and activities.

Said the great Hindu sage, Manu, "He who in his own soul perceives the Supreme Soul in all beings, and acquires equanimity toward them all, attains the highest bliss." It was Athanasius who said, "Even we may become Gods walking about in the flesh. The same great truth we are considering is the one that runs through the life and the teachings of Guatama, who became the Buddha. "People are in bondage," said he, "because they have not yet removed the idea of I." To do away with all sense of separateness, and to recognize the oneness of the self with the Infinite, is the spirit that breathes through all his teachings.

All the prophets, seers, sages, and saviours in the world's history became what they became, and consequently had the powers they had, through an entirely natural process. They all recognized and came into the conscious realization of their oneness with the Infinite Life. God is no respecter of persons. He doesn't create prophets, seers, sages, and saviours as such. He creates men. But here and there one recognizes his true identity, recognizes the oneness of his life with the Source whence it came. He lives in the realization of this oneness, and in turn becomes a prophet, seer, sage, or saviour.—*In Tune with the Infinite*

The Creative Power Of Thought

Of the vital power of thought and the interior forces in moulding conditions, and more, of the supremacy of thought over all conditions, the world has scarcely the faintest grasp, not to say even idea, as yet. The fact that thoughts are forces, and that through them we have creative power, is one of the most vital facts of the universe, the most vital fact of man's being. And through this instrumentality we have in our grasp and as our rightful heritage, the power of making life and all its manifold conditions exactly what we will.

Through our thought-forces we have creative power, not in a figurative sense, but in reality. Everything in the material universe about us had its origin first in spirit, in thought, and from this it took its form. The very world in which we live, with all its manifold wonders and sublime manifestations, is the result of the energies of the Divine Intelligence or Mind, — God, or whatever term it comes convenient for each one to use. And God said, Let there be, and there was, —the material world, at least the material manifestation of it, literally spoken into existence, the spoken word, however, but the outward manifestation of the interior forces of the Supreme Intelligence.

Every castle the world has ever seen was first an ideal in the architect's mind. Every statue was first an ideal in the sculptor's mind. Every piece of mechanism the world has ever known was first formed in the mind of the inventor. Here it was given birth to. These same mind-forces then dictated to and sent the energy into the hand that drew the model, and then again dictated to and sent the energy into the hands whereby the first instrument was clothed in the material form of metal or of wood. The lower negative always gives way to the higher when made positive. Mind is positive: matter is negative.

Each individual life is a part of, and hence is one with, the Infinite Life; and the highest intelligence and power belongs to each in just the degree that he recognizes his oneness and lays claim to and uses it. The power of the word is not merely an idle phrase or form of expression. It is a real mental, spiritual, scientific fact, and can become vital and powerful in your hands and in mine in just the degree that we understand the omnipotence of the thought forces and raise all to the higher planes.

The blind, the lame, the diseased, stood before Christ, who said, "receive thy sight, rise up and walk, or, be thou healed;" and lo! it was so. The spoken word, however, was but the outward expression and manifestation of His interior thought forces, the power and potency of which He so thoroughly knew. But the laws governing them are the same today as they were then, and it lies in our power to use them the same as it lay in His.

The Drawing Power Of Mind

Each individual life, after it has reached a certain age or degree of intelligence, lives in the midst of the surroundings or environments of its own creation; and this by reason of that wonderful power, the drawing power of mind, which is continually operating in every life, whether it is conscious of it or not.

We are all living, so to speak, in a vast ocean of thought. The very atmosphere about us is charged with the thought-forces that are being continually sent out. When the thought-forces leave the brain, they go out upon the atmosphere, the subtle conducting ether, much the same as sound-waves go out. It is by virtue of this law that thought transference is possible, and has become an established scientific fact, by virtue of which a person can so direct his thought-forces that a person at a distance, and in a receptive attitude, can get the thought much the same as sound, for example, is conducted through the agency of a connecting medium. Even though the thoughts as they leave a particular person, are not consciously directed, they go out; and all may be influenced by them in a greater or less degree, each one in proportion as he or she is more or less sensitively organized, or in proportion as he or she is negative, and so open to forces and influences from without. The law operating here is one with that great law of the universe, — that like attracts like, so that one continually attracts to himself forces and influences most akin to those of his own life. And his own life is determined by the thoughts and emotions he habitually entertains, for each is building his world from within. As within, so without; cause, effect.

A stalk of wheat and a stalk of corn are growing side by side, within an inch of each other. The soil is the same for both; but the wheat converts the food it takes from the soil into wheat, the likeness of itself, while the corn converts the food it takes from the same soil into corn, the likeness of itself. What that which each has taken from the soil is converted into is determined by the soul, the interior life, the interior forces of each. This same grain taken as food by two persons will be converted into the body of a criminal in the one case, and into the body of a saint in the other, each after its kind; and its kind is determined by the inner life of each. And what again determines the inner life of each? The thoughts and emotions that are habitually entertained and that inevitably, sooner or later, manifest themselves in outer material form.

Thought is the great builder in human life: it is the determining factor. Continually think thoughts that are good, and your life will show forth in goodness, and your body in health and beauty. Continually think evil and your life will show forth in evil, and your body in weakness and repulsiveness. Think thoughts of love, and you will love and will be loved. Think thoughts of hatred, and you will hate and will be hated. Each follows its kind.

Creating One's Own Atmosphere

It is by virtue of this law that each person creates his own "atmosphere"; and this atmosphere is determined by the character of the thoughts he habitually entertains. It is, in fact, simply his thought atmosphere — the atmosphere which other people detect and are influenced by.

In this way each person creates the atmosphere of his own room; a family, the atmosphere of the house in which they live, so that the moment you enter the door you feel influences kindred to the thoughts and hence to the lives of those who dwell there. You get a feeling of peace and harmony or a feeling of disquietude and inharmony. You get a welcome, want-to-stay feeling or a cold, want-to-getaway feeling, according to their thought attitude toward you, even though but few words be spoken. So the characteristic mental states of a congregation of people who assemble there determine the atmosphere of any given assembly-place, church, or cathedral. Its inhabitants so make, so determine the atmosphere of a particular village or city. The sympathetic thoughts sent out by a vast amphitheatre of people, as they cheer a contestant, carry him to goals he never could reach by his own efforts alone. The same is true in regard to an orator and his audience.

Napoleon's army is in the East. The plague is beginning to make inroads into its ranks. Long lines of men are lying on cots and on the ground in an open space adjoining the army. Fear has taken a vital hold of all, and the men are continually being stricken. Look yonder: contrary to the earnest entreaties of his officers, who tell him that such exposure will mean sure death, Napoleon with a calm and dauntless look upon his face, with a firm and defiant step, is coming through these plague stricken ranks. He is going up to, talking with, touching the men; and, as they see him, there goes up a mighty shout, — The Emperor! the Emperor!, and from that hour the plague in its inroads is stopped. A marvellous example of the power of a man who, by his own dauntless courage, absolute fearlessness, and power of mind, could send out such forces that they in turn awakened kindred forces in the minds of thousands of others, which in turn dominate their very bodies, so that the plague, and even death itself, is driven from the field. One of the grandest examples of a man of the most mighty and tremendous mind and will power, and at the same time an example of one of the grandest failures, taking life in its totality, the world has ever seen.

We are all much more influenced by the thought-forces and mental states of those around us and of the world at large than we have even the slightest conception of. If not self-hypnotized into certain beliefs and practices, we are, so to speak, semi-hypnotized through the influence of the thoughts of others, even though unconsciously both on their part and on ours. We are so influenced and enslaved in just the degree that we fail to recognize the power and omnipotence of our own forces, and so become slaves to custom, conventionality, the opinions of others, and so in like proportion lose our own individuality and powers.

Each is building his world from within, and, if outside forces play, it is because he allows them to play; and he has it in his own power to determine whether these shall be positive, uplifting, ennobling, strengthening, success-giving, or negative, degrading, weakening, failure-bringing. — *In Tune with the Infinite*

The Law Of Attraction Works Unceasingly

If one hold himself in the thought of poverty, he will be poor, and the chances are that he will remain in poverty. If he hold himself, whatever present conditions may be, continually in the thought of prosperity, he sets into operation forces that will sooner or later bring him into prosperous conditions. The law of attraction works unceasingly throughout the universe, and the one great and never changing fact in connection with it is, as we have found, that like attracts like. If we are one with this Infinite Power, this source of all things, then in the degree that we live in the realization of this oneness, in that degree do we actualize in our selves a power that will bring to us an abundance of all things that it is desirable for us to have. In this way we come into possession of a power where by we can actualize at all times those conditions that we desire.

As all truth exists now, and awaits simply our perception of it, so all things necessary for present needs exist now, and await simply the power in us to appropriate them. God holds all things in His hands. His constant word is, My child, acknowledge me in all your ways, and in the degree that you do this, in the degree that you live this, then what is mine is yours. Jehovah-jireh, — the Lord will provide. "He giveth to all men liberally and upbraideth not." He giveth liberally to all men who put themselves in the right attitude to receive from Him. He forces no good things upon anyone.

The old and somewhat prevalent idea of godliness and poverty has absolutely no basis for its existence, and the sooner we get away from it the better. It had its birth in the same way that the idea of asceticism came into existence, when the idea prevailed that there was necessarily a warfare between the flesh and the spirit. It had its origin therefore in the minds of those who had a distorted, a one-sided view of life. True godliness is in a sense the same as true wisdom. The one who is truly wise, and who uses the forces and powers with which he is endowed, to him the great universe always opens her treasure house.

Are you out of a situation? Let the fear that you will not get another take hold of and dominate you, and the chances are that it may be a long time before you will get another, or the one that you do get may be a very poor one indeed. Whatever the circumstances, you must realize that you have within you forces and powers that you can set into operation that will triumph over any and all apparent or temporary losses. Set these forces into operation and you will then be placing a magnet that will draw to you a situation that may be far better than the one you have lost, and the time may soon come when you will be even thankful that you lost the old one.

Recognize, working in and through you, the same Infinite Power that creates and governs all things in the universe, the same Infinite Power that governs the endless systems of worlds in space. Send out your thought, — thought is a force, and it has occult power of unknown proportions when rightly used and wisely directed, —send out your thought that the right situation or the right work will come to you at the right time, in the right way, and that you will recognize it when it comes. Hold to this thought, never allow it to weaken, hold to it, and continually water it with firm expectation. You in this way put your advertisement into a psychical, a spiritual newspaper, a paper that has not a limited circulation, but one that will make its way not only to the utmost bounds of the earth, but of the very universe itself. It is an advertisement, moreover, which if rightly placed on your part, will be far more effective than any advertisement you could possibly put into any printed sheet, no matter what claims are made in regard to its being "the great advertising medium."

In the degree that you come into this realization and live in harmony with the higher laws and forces, in that degree will you be able to do this effectively. If you wish to look through the "want" columns of the newspapers, then do it, but not in the ordinary way. Put the higher forces into operation and thus place it on a higher basis.

If you get the situation and it does not prove to be exactly what you want, if you feel that you are capable of filling a better one, then the moment you enter upon it take the attitude of mind that this situation is the stepping-stone that will lead you to one that will be still better. Hold this thought steadily, affirm it, believe it, expect it, and all the time be faithful, absolutely faithful to the situation in which you are at present placed. If you are not faithful to it then the chances are that it will not be the stepping-stone to something better, but to something poorer. If you are faithful to it, the time may soon come when you will be glad and thankful, when you will rejoice, that you lost your old position.—*In Tune with the Infinite*

The Law Of Prosperity

This is the law of prosperity: When apparent adversity comes, be not cast down by it, but make the best of it, and always look forward for better things, for conditions more prosperous. To hold yourself in this attitude of mind is to set into operation subtle, silent, and irresistible forces that sooner or later will actualize in material form that which is today merely an idea. But ideas have mystical power, and ideas, when rightly planted and rightly tended, are the seeds that actualize material conditions.

Never give a moment to complaint, but utilize the time that would otherwise be spent in this way in looking forward and actualizing the conditions you desire. Suggest prosperity to yourself. See yourself in a prosperous condition. Affirm that you will before long be in a prosperous condition. Affirm it calmly and quietly, but strongly and confidently. Believe it, believe it absolutely. Expect it, — keep it continually watered with expectation. You thus make yourself a magnet to attract the things that you desire. Don't be afraid to suggest, to affirm these things, for by so doing you put forth an ideal which will begin to clothe itself in material form. In this way you are utilizing agents among the most subtle and powerful in the universe. If you are particularly desirous for anything that you feel it is good and right for you to have, something that will broaden your life or that will increase your usefulness to others, simply hold the thought that at the right time, in the right way, and through the right instrumentality, there will come to you or there will open up for you the way whereby you can attain what you desire.

Don't fold your hands and expect to see things drop into your lap, but set into operation the higher forces and then take hold of the first thing that offers itself. Do what your hands find to do, and do it well. If this work is not thoroughly satisfactory to you, then affirm, believe, and expect that it is the agency that will lead you to something better. "The basis for attracting the best of all the world can give to you is to first surround, own, and live in these things in mind, or what is falsely called imagination. All so-called imaginings are realities and forces of unseen element. Live in mind in a palace and gradually palatial surroundings will gravitate to you. But so living is not pining, or longing, or complainingly wishing. It is when you are 'down in the world,' calmly and persistently seeing yourself as up. It is when you are now compelled to eat from a tin plate, regarding that tin plate as only the certain step to one of silver. It is not envying and growling at other people who have silver plate. That growling is just so much capital stock taken from the bank account of mental force."

A friend who knows the power of the interior forces, and whose life is guided in every detail by them, has given a suggestion in this form: When you are in the arms of the bear, even though he is hugging you, look him in the face and laugh, but all the time keep your eye on the bull. If you allow all of your attention to be given to the work of the bear, the bull may get entirely out of your sight. In other words, if you yield to adversity the chances are that it will master you, but if you recognize in yourself the power of mastery over conditions then adversity will yield to you, and will be changed into prosperity. If when it comes you calmly and quietly recognize it, and use the time that might otherwise be spent in regrets, and fears, and forebodings, in setting into operation the powerful forces within you, it will soon take its leave.

Faith, absolute dogmatic faith, is the only law of true success. When we recognize the fact that a man carries his success or his failure with him, and that it does not depend upon outside conditions, we will come into the possession of powers that will quickly change outside conditions into agencies that make for success. When we come into this higher realization and bring our lives into complete harmony with the higher laws, we will then be able so to focus and direct the awakened interior forces, that they will go out and return laden with that for which they are sent. We will then be great enough to attract success, and it will not always be apparently just a little ways ahead. We can then establish in ourselves a centre so strong that instead of running hither and thither for this or that, we can stay at home and draw to us the conditions we desire. If we firmly establish and hold to this centre, things will seem continually to come our way.—*In Tune with the Infinite*

The Law Of Habit-Forming

Have we it within our power to determine at all times what types of habits shall take form in our lives? In other words, is habit-forming, character-building, a matter of mere chance, or have we it within our own control? We have, entirely and absolutely.

For there is a simple, natural, and thoroughly scientific method that all should know. A method whereby old, undesirable, earth-binding habits can be broken, and new, desirable, heaven-lifting habits can be acquired, — a method whereby life in part or in its totality can be changed, provided one is sufficiently in earnest to know, and, knowing it, to apply the law.

Thought is the force underlying all. And what do we mean by this? Simply this: Your every act — every conscious act — is preceded by a thought. Your dominating thoughts determine your dominating actions. The acts repeated crystallize themselves into the habit. The aggregate of your habits is your character. Whatever, then, you would have your acts, you must look well to the character of the thought you entertain. Whatever act you would not do, —habit you would not acquire you must look well to it that you do not entertain the type of thought that will give birth to this act, this habit . It is a simple psychological law that any type of thought, if entertained for a sufficient length of time, will, by and by, reach the motor tracks of the brain, and finally burst forth into action. Murder can be and many times is committed in this way, the same as all undesirable things are done. On the other hand, the greatest powers are grown, the most God-like characteristics are engendered, the most heroic acts are performed in the same way.

The thing clearly to understand is this: That the thought is always parent to the act. Now, we have it entirely in our own hands to determine exactly what thoughts we entertain. In the realm of our own minds we have absolute control, or we should have, and if at any time we have not, then there is a method by which we can gain control, and in the realm of the mind become thorough masters.

Here let us refer to that law of the mind which is the same as is the law in connection with the reflex nerve system of the body, the law which says that whenever one does a certain thing in a certain way it is easier to do the same thing in the same way the next time, and still easier the next, and the next, and the next, until in time it comes to pass that no effort is required, or no effort worth speaking of; but on the contrary, to do the opposite would require the effort. The mind carries with it the power that perpetuates its own type of thought, the same as the body carries with it through the reflex nerve system the power which perpetuates and makes continually easier its own particular acts. Thus a simple effort to control one's thoughts, a simple setting about it, even if at first failure is the result, and even if for a time failure seems to be about the only result, will in time, sooner or later, bring him to the point of easy, full, and complete control.

Each one, then, can grow the power of determining, controlling his thought, the power of determining what types of thought he shall and what types he shall not entertain. For let us never part in mind with this fact, that every earnest effort along any line makes the end aimed at just a little easier for each succeeding effort, even if, as has been said, apparent failure is the result of the earlier efforts. This is a case where even failure is success, for the failure is not in the effort, and every earnest effort adds an increment of power that will eventually accomplish the end aimed at.—*Character-Building Thought Power*

Actualizing One's Ideals

There is nothing more true in connection with human life than that we grow into the likeness of those things we contemplate. Literally and scientifically and necessarily true is it that, "as a man thinketh in his heart, so is he." The "is" part is his character. His character is the sum total of his habits. His habits have been formed by his conscious acts; but every conscious act is, as we have found, preceded by a thought. And so we have it — thought on the one hand, character, life, destiny on the other. And simple it becomes when we bear in mind that it is simply the thought of the present moment, and the next moment when it is upon us, and then the next, and so on through all time.

One can in this way attain to whatever ideals he would attain to. Two steps are necessary: first, as the days pass, to form one's ideals; and second, to follow them continually whatever may arise, wherever they may lead him. Always remember that the great and strong character is the one who is ever ready to sacrifice the present pleasure for the future good. He who will thus follow his highest ideals as they present themselves to him day after day, year after year, will find that as Dante, following his beloved from world to world, finally found her at the gates of Paradise, so he will find himself eventually at the same gates. Life is not, we may say, for mere passing pleasure, but for the highest unfoldment that one can attain to, the noblest character that one can grow, and for the greatest service that one can render to all mankind. In this, however, we will find the highest pleasure, for in this the only real pleasure lies.

The question is not, What are the conditions in our lives? but, How do we meet the conditions that we find there? And whatever the conditions are, it is unwise and profitless to look upon them, even if they are conditions that we would have otherwise, in the attitude of complaint, for complaint will bring depression, and depression will weaken and possibly even kill the spirit that would engender the power that would enable us to bring into our lives an entirely new set of conditions.

Each one is so apt to think that his own conditions, his own trials or troubles or sorrows, or his own struggles, as the case may be, are greater than those of the great mass of mankind, or possibly greater than those of any one else in the world. He forgets that each one has his own peculiar trials or troubles or sorrows to bear, or struggles in habits to overcome, and that his is but the common lot of all the human race. We are apt to make the mistake in this — in that we see and feel keenly our own trials, or adverse conditions, or characteristics to be overcome, while those of others we do not see so clearly, and hence we are apt to think that they are not at all equal to our own.

Each has his own problems to work out. Each must work out his own problems. Each must grow the insight that will enable him to see what the causes are that have brought the unfavorable conditions into his life; each must grow the strength that will enable him to face these conditions, and to set into operation forces that will bring about a different set of conditions. We may be of aid to one another by way of suggestion, by way of bringing to one another a knowledge of certain higher laws and forces, — laws and forces that will make it easier to do that which we Character Building Thought Power would do. The doing, however, must be done by each one for himself.—*Character Building Thought Power*

Faith And Prayer — Their Nature

What, shall we ask, is the place, what the value, of prayer? Prayer, as every act of devotion, brings us into an ever greater conscious harmony with the Infinite, the one pearl of great price; for it is this harmony which brings all other things. Prayer is the soul's sincere desire and thus is its own answer, as the sincere desire made active and accompanied by faith sooner or later gives place to realization;

for faith is an invisible and invincible magnet, and attracts to itself whatever it fervently desires and calmly and persistently expects. This is absolute, and the results will be absolute in exact proportion as this operation of the thought forces, as this faith is absolute, and relative in exact proportion as it is relative.

The Master said, "What things soever ye desire, when ye pray, believe that ye receive them and ye shall have them." Can any law be more clearly enunciated, can anything be more definite and more absolute than this? According to thy faith be it unto thee. Do we at times fail in obtaining the results we desire? The fault, the failure, lies not in the law but in ourselves. Regarded in its right and true light, than prayer there is nothing more scientific, nothing more valuable, nothing more effective.

This conscious realization of oneness with the Infinite Life is of all things the one thing to be desired; for, when this oneness is realized and lived in, all other things follow in its train, there are no desires that shall not be realized, for God has planted in the human breast no desire without its corresponding means of realization. No harm can come nigh, nothing can touch us, there will be nothing to fear; for we shall thus attract only the good. And whatever changes time may bring, understanding the law, we shall always expect something better, and thus, set into operation the forces that will attract that something, realizing that many times angels go out that archangels may enter in; and this is always true in the case of the life of this higher realization. And why should we have any fear whatever, — fear even for the nation as is many times expressed? God is behind His world, in love and with infinite care and watchfulness working out His great and almighty plans;

and whatever plans men may devise, He will when the time is ripe either frustrate and shatter, or aid and push through to their most perfect culmination, —frustrate and shatter if contrary to, aid and actualize if in harmony with His.

These facts, the facts relating to the powers that come with the higher awakening, have been dealt with somewhat fully, to show that the matters along the lines of man's interior, intuitive, spiritual, thought, soul life, instead of being, as they are so many times regarded, merely indefinite, sentimental, or impractical, are, on the contrary, powerfully, omnipotently real, and are of all practical things in the world the most practical, and, in the truest and deepest sense, the only truly practical things there are. And pre-eminently is this true when we look with a long range of vision, past the mere today, to the final outcome, to the time when that transition we are accustomed to call death takes place, and all accumulations and possessions material are left behind, and the soul takes with it only the unfoldment and growth of the real life; and unless it has this, when all else must be left behind, it goes out poor indeed. And a most wonderful and beautiful fact of it all is this: that all growth, all advancement, all attainment made along the lines of the spiritual, the soul, the real life, is so much made forever, and can never be lost.—*In Tune with the Infinite*

The Petty Personal And The Larger Universal

When the step from the personal to the impersonal, from the personal, the individual, to the universal, is once made, the great solution of life has come; and by this same step one enters at once into the realm of all power. When this is done, and one fully realizes the fact that the greatest life is the life spent in the service of all mankind, and then when he vitally grasps that great eternal principle of right, of truth, of justice, that runs through all the universe, and which, though temporarily it may seem to be perverted, always and with never an exception eventually prevails, and that with an omnipotent power, he then holds the key to all situations. A king of this nature goes about his work absolutely regardless of what men may say or hear or think or do; for he himself has absolutely nothing to gain or nothing to lose, and nothing of this nature can come near him or touch him, for he is standing not in the personal, but in the universal. He is then in God's work, and the very God-powers are his, and it seems as if the very angels of heaven come to minister unto him and to move things his way; and this is true, very true, for he himself is simply moving God's way, and when this is so, the certainty of the outcome is absolute.

How often did the Master say, "I seek not to do mine own will, but the will of the Father who sent me"! Here is the world's great example of the life out of the personal and in the universal, hence His great power. The same has been true of all the saviours, the prophets, the seers, the sages, and the leaders in the world's history, of all of truly great and lasting power.

He who would then come into the secret of power must come from the personal into the universal, and with this comes not only great power, but also freedom from the vexations and perplexities that rise from the misconstruing of motives, the opinions of others; for such a one cares nothing as to what men may say, or hear, or think, or do, so long as he is true to the great principles of right and truth before him. And, if we will search carefully, we shall find that practically all the perplexities and difficulties of life have their origin on the side of the personal.

Much is said to young men today about success in life — success generally though, as the world calls success. It is well, however, always to bear in mind the fact that there is a success which is a miserable, a deplorable failure; while, on the other hand, there is a failure which is a grand, a noble, a God-like success. And one crying need of the age is that young men be taught the true dignity, nobility, and power of such a failure, — such a failure in the eyes of the world today, but such a success in the eyes of God and the coming ages. When this is done, there will be among us more prophets, more saviours, more men of grand and noble stature, who with a firm and steady hand will hold the lighted torch of true advancement high up among the people; and they will be those whom the people will gladly follow, for they will be those who will speak and move with authority, true sons of God, true brothers of men. A man may make his millions and his life be a failure still.—*In Tune with the Infinite*

The Poem Hangs On The Berry Bush

To live undisturbed by passing occurrences you must first find your own centre. You must then be firm in your own centre, and so rule the world from within. He who does not himself condition circumstances allows the process to be reversed, and becomes a conditioned circumstance. Find your centre and live in it. Surrender it to no person, to no thing. In the degree that you do this will you find yourself growing stronger and stronger in it. And how can one find his centre? By realizing his oneness with the Infinite Power, and by living continually in this realization.

But if you do not rule from your own centre, if you invest this or that with the power of bringing you annoyance, or evil, or harm, then take what it brings, but cease your railings against the eternal goodness and beneficence of all things.

"I swear the earth shall surely be complete, To him or her who shall be complete; The earth remains jagged and broken, Only to him who remains jagged and broken."

If the windows of your soul are dirty and streaked, covered with matter foreign to them, then the world as you look out of them will be to you dirty and streaked and out of order. Cease your complainings, however; keep your pessimism, your " poor, unfortunate me " to yourself, lest you betray the fact that your windows are badly in need of something. But know that your friend, who keeps his windows clean, that the Eternal Sun may illumine all within and make visible all without, — know that he lives in a different world from yours.

Then, go wash your windows, and instead of longing for some other world, you will discover the wonderful beauties of this world; and if you don't find transcendent beauties on every hand here, the chances are that: you will never find them anywhere.

"The poem hangs on the berry-bush, When comes the poet's eye, And the whole street is a masquerade, When Shakespeare passes by."

This same Shakespeare, whose mere passing causes all this commotion, is the one who put into the mouth of one of his creations the words: "The fault, dear Brutus, is not in our stars, but in ourselves, that we are underlings." And the great work of his own life is right good evidence that he realized full well the truth of the facts we are considering. And again he gave us a great truth in keeping with what we are considering when he said: "Our doubts are traitors, And make us lose the good we oft might win, By fearing to attempt."

There is probably no agent that brings us more undesirable conditions than fear. We should live in fear of nothing, nor will we when we come fully to know ourselves. An old French proverb runs:

"Some of your griefs you have cured, And the sharpest you still have survived; But what torments of pain you endured, From evils that never arrived."

Fear and lack of faith go hand in hand. The one is born of the other. Tell me how much one is given to fear, and I will tell you how much he lacks in faith. Fear is a most expensive guest to entertain, the same as worry is: so expensive are they that no one can afford to entertain them. We invite what we fear, the same as, by a different attitude of mind, we invite and attract the influences and conditions we desire. The mind dominated by fear opens the door for the entrance of the very things, for the actualization of the very conditions it fears.

"Where are you going? " asked an Eastern pilgrim on meeting the plague one day. " I am going to Bagdad to kill five thousand people," was the reply. A few days later the same pilgrim met the plague returning. "You told me you were going to Baghdad to kill five thousand people," said he, "but instead, you killed fifty thousand." "No," said the plague, "I killed only five thousand, as I told you I would; the others died of fright.

Fear can paralyze every muscle in the body. Fear affects the flow of the blood, likewise the normal and healthy action of all the life forces. Fear can make the body rigid, motionless, and powerless to move.—*In Tune with the Infinite*

The Influence Of Our Prevailing Mental States Upon Others

Not only do we attract to ourselves the things we fear, but we also aid in attracting to others the conditions we in our own minds hold them in fear of. This we do in proportion to the strength of our own thought, and in the degree that they are sensitively organized and so influenced by our thought, and this, although it be unconscious both on their part and on ours.

Children, and especially when very young, are, generally speaking, more sensitive to their surrounding influences than grown people are. Some are veritable little sensitive plates, registering the influences about them, and embodying them as they grow. How careful in their prevailing mental states then should be those who have them in charge, and especially how careful should a mother be during the time she is carrying the child, and when every thought, every mental as well as emotional state has its direct influence upon the life of the unborn child. Let parents be careful how they hold a child, either younger or older, in the thought of fear. This is many times done, unwittingly on their part, through anxiety, and at times through what might well be termed over-care, which is fully as bad as under-care.

I know of a number of cases where a child has been so continually held in the thought of fear lest this or that condition come upon him, that the very things that were feared have been drawn to him, which probably otherwise never would have come at all. Many times there has been no adequate basis for the fear. In case there is a basis, then far wiser is it to take exactly the opposite attitude, so as to neutralize the force at work, and then to hold the child in the thought of wisdom and strength that it may be able to meet the condition and master it, instead of being mastered by it.

But a day or two ago a friend was telling me of an experience of his own life in this connection. At a period when he was having a terrific struggle with a certain habit, he was so continually held in the thought of fear by his mother and the young lady to whom he was engaged, — the engagement to be consummated at the end of a certain period, the time depending on his proving his mastery, — that he, very sensitively organized, continually felt the depressing and weakening effects of their negative thoughts. He could always tell exactly how they felt toward him; he was continually influenced and weakened by their fear, by their questionings, by their suspicions, all of which had the effect of lessening the sense of his own power, all of which had an endeavor-paralyzing influence upon him. And so instead of their begetting courage and strength in him, they brought him to a still greater realization of his own weakness and the almost worthless use of struggle.

Here were two who loved him dearly, and who would have done anything and everything to help him gain the mastery, but who, ignorant of the silent, subtle, ever-working and all-telling power of the thought forces, instead of imparting to him courage, instead of adding to his strength, disarmed him of this, and then added an additional weakness from without. In this way the battle for him was made harder in a three-fold degree.

Fear and worry and all kindred mental states are too espensive for any person, man, woman, or child, to entertain or indulge in. Fear paralyzes healthy action, worry corrodes and pulls down the organism, and will finally tear it to pieces. Nothing is to be gained by it, but everything to be lost. Long-continued grief at any loss will do the same. Each brings its own peculiar type of ailment. An inordinate love of gain, a close-fisted, hoarding disposition will have kindred effects. Anger, jealousy, malice, continual fault-finding, lust, has each its own peculiar corroding, weakening, tearing down effects.

We shall find that not only are happiness and prosperity concomitants of righteousness, — living in harmony with the higher laws, but bodily health as well. The great Hebrew seer enunciated a wonderful chemistry of life when he said, —" As righteousness tendeth to life, so he that pursueth evil, pursueth it to his own death." On the other hand, "In the way of righteousness is life; and in the pathway thereof there is no death." The time will come when it will be seen that this means far more than most people dare even to think as yet. "It rests with man to say whether his soul shall be housed in a stately mansion of ever-growing splendor and beauty, or in a hovel of his own building, — a hovel at last ruined and abandoned to decay."

The bodies of almost untold numbers, living their one-sided, unbalanced lives, are every year, through these influences, weakening and falling by the wayside long before their time. Poor, poor houses! Intended to be beautiful temples, brought to desolation by their ignorant, reckless, deluded tenants. Poor houses!—*In Tune with the Infinite*

Saviours One Of Another

And in the same sense we are all the saviours one of another, or may become so. A sudden emergency arises, and I stand faltering and weak with fear. My friend beside me is strong and fearless. He sees the emergency. He summons up all the latent powers within him, and springs forth to meet it. This sublime example arouses me, calls my latent powers into activity, when but for him I might not have known them there. I follow his example. I now know my powers, and know them forever after. Thus, in this, my friend has become my saviour.

I am weak in some point of character, — vacillating, yielding, stumbling, falling, continually eating the bitter fruit of it all. My friend is strong, he has gained thorough self-mastery. The majesty and beauty of power are upon his brow. I see his example, I love his life, I am influenced by his power. My soul longs and cries out for the same. A supreme effort of will — that imperial master that will take one anywhere when rightly directed — arises within me, it is born at last, and it calls all the soul's latent powers into activity: and instead of stumbling I stand firm, instead of giving over in weakness I stand firm and master, I enter into the joys of full self-mastery, and through this into the mastery of all things besides. And thus my friend has again become my saviour.

With the new power I have acquired through the example and influence of my saviour-friend, I, in turn, stand before a friend who is struggling, who is stumbling and in despair. He sees, he feels, the power of my strength. He longs for, his soul cries out for the same. His interior forces are called into activity, he now knows his powers; and instead of the slave, he becomes the master, and thus I, in turn, have become his saviour. Oh, the wonderful sense of sublimity, the mighty feelings of responsibility, the deep sense of power and peace the recognition of this fact should bring to each and all. God works through the instrumentality of human agency. Then forever away with that old, shrivelling, weakening, dying, and devilish idea that we are poor worms of the dust! We may or we may not be: it all depends upon the self. The moment we believe we are we become such; and as long as we hold to the belief we will be held to this identity, and will act and live as such. The moment, however, we recognize our divinity, our higher, our God-selves, and the fact that we are the saviours of our fellow-men, we become saviours, and stand and move in the midst of a majesty and beauty and power that of itself proclaims us as such.

There is a prevalent idea to the effect that overcoming in this sense necessarily implies more or less of a giving up, —that it means something possibly on the order of asceticism. On the contrary, the highest, truest, keenest pleasures the human soul can know, it finds only after the higher is entered upon and has commenced its work of mastery; and, instead of there being a giving up of any kind, there is a great law which says that the lower always and of its own accord falls away before the higher.—*In Tune with the Infinite*

Not Repression, But Self-Mastery

From what has been said let it not be inferred that the body, the physical, material life is to be despised or looked down upon. This, rather let it be said, is one of the crying errors of the times, and prolific of a vast amount of error, suffering, and shame. On the contrary, it should be thought all the more highly of: it should be loved and developed to its highest perfections, beauties, and powers. God gave us the body not in vain. It is just as holy and beautiful as the spirit itself. It is merely the outward material manifestation of the individualized spirit; and we by our hourly thoughts and emotions are building it, are determining its conditions, its structure, and appearance.

Every part, every organ, every function of the body is just as clean, just as beautiful, just as sweet, and just as holy as every other part; and it is only by virtue of man's perverted ways of looking at some that they become otherwise, and the moment they so become, abuses, ill uses, suffering, and shame creep in.

Not repression, but elevation. Would that this could be repeated a thousand times over! Not repression, but elevation. Every part, every organ, every function of the body is given for use, but not for misuse or abuse; and the moment the latter takes place in connection with any function it loses its higher powers of use, and there goes with this the higher powers of true enjoyment.

No, a knowledge of the spiritual realities of life prohibits asceticism, repression, the same as it prohibits license and perverted use. To err on the one side is just as contrary to the ideal life as to err on the other. All things are for a purpose, all should be used and enjoyed; but all should be rightly used, that they may be fully enjoyed.

It is the threefold life and development that is wanted, — physical, mental, spiritual. This gives the rounded life, and he or she who fails in any one comes short of the perfect whole. The physical has its uses just the same and is just as important as the others. The great secret of the highly successful life is, however, to infuse the mental and the physical with the spiritual; in other words, to spiritualize all, and so raise all to the highest possibilities and powers.

It is the all-around, fully developed we want, —not the ethereal, pale-blooded man and woman, but the man and woman of flesh and blood, for action and service here and now, — the man and woman strong and powerful, with all the faculties and functions fully unfolded and used, all in a royal and bounding condition, but all rightly subordinated. The man and the woman of this kind, with the imperial hand of mastery upon all, — standing, moving thus like a king, nay, like a very God, — such is the man and such is the woman of power. Such is the ideal life: anything else is one-sided, and falls short of it.—*In Tune with the Infinite*

Thoughts Are Forces

Thought is at the bottom of all progress or retrogression, of all success or failure, of all that is desirable or undesirable in human life. The type of thought we entertain both creates and draws conditions that crystallize about it, conditions exactly the same in nature as is the thought that gives them form. Thoughts are forces, and each creates of its kind, whether we realize it or not. The great law of the drawing power of the mind, which says that like creates like, and that like attracts like, is continually working in every human life, for it is one of the great immutable laws of the universe. For one to take time to see clearly the things he would attain to, and then to hold that ideal steadily and continually before his mind, never allowing faith — his positive thought-forces — to give way to or to be neutralized by doubts and fears, and then to set about doing each day what his hands find to do, never complaining, but spending the time that he would otherwise spend in complaint in focusing his thought-forces upon the ideal that his mind has built, will sooner or later bring about the full materialization of that for which he sets out.

There are those who, when they begin to grasp the fact that there is what we may term a "science of thought," who, when they begin to realize that through the instrumentality of our interior, spiritual thought-forces we have the power of gradually moulding the everyday conditions of life as we would have them, in their early enthusiasm are not able to see results as quickly as they expect, and are apt to think, therefore, that after all there is not very much in that which has but newly come to their knowledge. They must remember, however, that in endeavoring to overcome an old or to grow a new habit, everything cannot be done all at once.

In the degree that we attempt to use the thought-forces do we continually become able to use them more effectively. Progress is slow at first, more rapid as we proceed. Power grows by using, or, in other words, using brings a continually increasing power. This is governed by law the same as are all things in our lives, and all things in the universe about us. Every act and advancement made by the musician is in full accordance with law. No one commencing the study of music can, for example, sit down to the piano and play the piece of a master at the first effort. He must not conclude, however, nor does he conclude, that the piece of the master cannot be played by him, or, for that matter, by anyone.

He begins to practice the piece. The law of the mind that we have already noticed comes to his aid, whereby his mind follows the music more readily, more rapidly, and more surely each succeeding time, and there also comes into operation and to his aid the law underlying the action of the reflex nerve system of the body, which we have also noticed, whereby his fingers coordinate their movements with the movements of his mind, more readily, more rapidly, and more accurately each succeeding time; until by and by the time comes when that which he stumbles through at first, that in which there is no harmony, nothing but discord, finally reveals itself as the music of the master, the music that thrills and moves masses of men and women. So it is in the use of the thought-forces. It is the reiteration, the constant reiteration of the thought that grows the power of continually stronger thought-focusing, and that finally brings manifestation.—*Character-Building Thought Power*

All Life From Within

All life is from within out. This is something that cannot be reiterated too often. The springs of life are all from within. This being true, it would be well for us to give more time to the inner life than we are accustomed to give to it, especially in this Western World.

There is nothing that will bring us such abundant returns as to take a little time in the quiet each day of our lives. We need this to get the kinks out of our minds and hence out of our lives. We need this to form better the higher ideals of life. We need this in order to see clearly in mind the things upon which we would concentrate and focus the thought-forces. We need this in order to make continually anew and to keep our conscious connection with the Infinite. We need this in order that the rush and hurry of our everyday life does not keep us away from the conscious realization of the fact that the spirit of Infinite life and power that is back of all, working in and through all, the life of all, is the life of our life, and the source of our power; and that outside of this we have no life and we have no power. To realize this fact fully, and to live in it consciously at all times, is to find the kingdom of God, which is essentially an inner kingdom, and can never be anything else.

The kingdom of heaven is to be found only within, and is done once for all, and in a manner in which it cannot otherwise be done, when we come into the conscious, living realization of the fact that in our real selves we are essentially one with the Divine life, and open ourselves continually so that this Divine life can speak to and manifest through us. In this way we come into the condition where we are continually walking with God. In this way the consciousness of God becomes a living reality in our lives; and in the degree in which it becomes a reality does it bring us into the realization of continually increasing wisdom, insight, and power. This consciousness of God in the soul of man is the essence, indeed the sum and substance of all religion. This identifies religion with every act and every moment of everyday life. That which does not identify itself with every moment of every day and with every act of life is religion in name only and not in reality.

It is the attitude of the child that is necessary before we can enter into the kingdom of heaven. As it was said by Jesus of Nazareth, "Except ye become as little children, ye cannot enter into the kingdom of heaven." For we then realize that of ourselves we can do nothing but that it is only as we realize that it is the Divine life and power working, within us, and it is only as we open ourselves that it may work through us, that we are or can do anything. It is thus that the simple life, which is essentially the life of the greatest enjoyment and the greatest attainment, is entered upon.

In the Orient the people as a class take far more time in the quiet, in the silence, than we take. Some of them carry this possibly to as great an extreme as we carry the opposite, with the result that they do not actualize and objectify in the outer life the things they dream in the inner life. We give so much time to the activities of the outer life that we do not take sufficient time in the quiet to form in the inner, spiritual thought-life the ideals and the conditions that we would have actualized and manifested in the outer life. The result is that we take life in a kind of haphazard way, taking it as it comes, thinking not very much about it until, perhaps, pushed by some bitter experiences, instead of moulding it, through the agency of the inner forces, exactly as we would have it. We need to strike the happy balance between the custom in this respect of the Eastern and Western worlds, and go to the extreme of neither the one nor the other.

If the Oriental would do his contemplating, and then get up and do his work, he would be in a better condition; he would be living a more normal and satisfactory life. If we in the Occident would take more time from the rush and activity of life for contemplation, for meditation, for idealization, for becoming acquainted with our real selves, and then go about our work manifesting the powers of our real selves, we would be far better off, because we would be living a more natural, a more normal life. To find one's centre, to become centered in the Infinite, is the first great essential of every satisfactory life; and then to go out, thinking, speaking, working, loving, living, from this centre.—*Character-Building Thought Power*

Heredity And The Higher Power

In the highest character-building, such as we have been considering, there are those who feel they are handicapped by what we term heredity. In a sense they are right; in another sense they are totally wrong. It is along the same lines as the thought which many before us had inculcated in them through the couplet in the New England Primer: "In Adam's fall, we sinned all." Now, in the first place, it is rather hard to understand the justice of this if it is true. In the second place, it is rather hard to understand why it is true. And in the third place there is no truth in it at all.

We are now dealing with the real essential self, and, however old Adam is, God is eternal. This means you; it means me; it means every human soul. When we fully realize this fact we see that heredity is a reed that is easily broken. The life of everyone is in his own hands and he can make it in character, in attainment, in power, in divine self-realization, and hence in influence, exactly what he wills to make it. All things that he most fondly dreams of are his, or may become so if he is truly in earnest; and as he rises more and more to his ideal, and grows in the strength and influence of his character, he becomes an example and an inspiration to all with whom he comes in contact; so that through him the weak and faltering are encouraged and strengthened; so that those of low ideals and of a low type of life instinctively and inevitably have their ideals raised, and the ideals of no one can be raised without its showing forth in his outer life.

As he advances in his grasp upon and understanding of the power and potency of the thought-forces, he finds that many times through the process of mental suggestion he can be of tremendous aid to one who is weak and struggling, by sending to him now and then, and by continually holding him in the highest thought, in the thought of the highest strength, wisdom, and love.

The one who takes sufficient time in the quiet mentally to form his ideals, sufficient time to make and to keep continually his conscious connection with the Infinite, with the Divine life and forces, is the one who is best adapted to the strenuous life. He it is who can go out and deal with sagacity and power with whatever issues may arise in the affairs of everyday life. He it is who is building not for the years, but for the centuries; not for time, but for the eternities. And he can go out knowing not wither he goes, knowing that the Divine life within him will never fail him, but will lead him on until he beholds the Father face to face. He is building for the centuries because only that which is the highest, the truest, the noblest, and best will abide the test of the centuries. He is building for eternity because when the transition we call death takes place, life, character, self-mastery, divine self-realization, — the only things that the soul when stripped of everything else takes with it he has in abundance. In life, or when the time of the transition to another form of life comes, he is never afraid, never fearful, because he knows and realizes that behind him, within him, beyond him, is the Infinite wisdom and love; and in this he is eternally centered, and from it he can never be separated. With Whittier he sings:

"I know not where His islands lift Their fronded palms in air; I only know I cannot drift Beyond His love and care."—*Character-Building Thought Power*

Castles In The Air

In our very laboratory experiments we are demonstrating the great fact that thoughts are forces. They have form, and duality, and substance, and power, and we are beginning to find that there is what we may term a science of thought.

Everything in the material universe about us, everything the universe has ever known, had its origin first in thought. From this it took its form. Every castle, every statue, every painting, every piece of mechanism, everything had its birth, its origin, first in the mind of the one who formed it before it received its material expression or embodiment. The Very universe in which we live is the result of the thought energies of God, the Infinite Spirit that is back of all. And if it is true, as we have found, that we in our true selves are in essence the same, and in this sense are one with the life of this Infinite Spirit, do we not then see that in the degree that we come into a vital realization of this stupendous fact, we, through the operation of our interior, spiritual, thought forces, have in like sense creative power?

Everything exists in the unseen before it is manifested or realized in the seen, and in this sense it is true that the unseen things are the real, while the things that are seen are the unreal. The unseen things are cause; the seen things are effect. The unseen things are the eternal; the seen things are the changing, the transient.

The "power of the word" is a literal scientific fact. Through the operation of our thought forces we have creative power. The spoken word is nothing more nor less than the outward expression of the workings of these interior forces. The spoken word is then, in a sense, the means whereby the thought-forces are focused and directed along any particular line; and this concentration, this giving them direction, is necessary before any outward or material manifestation of their power can become evident.

Much is said in regard to "building castles in the air," and one who is given to this building is not always looked upon with favour. But castles in the air are always necessary before we can have castles on the ground, before we can have castles in which to live. The trouble with the one who gives himself to building castles in the air is not that he builds them in the air, but that he does not go farther and actualize in life, in character, in material form, the castles he thus builds. He does part of the work, a very necessary part; but another equally necessary part remains still undone.

There is in connection with the thought-forces what we may term, the drawing power of mind, and the great law operating here is one with that great law of the universe, that like attracts like. We are continually attracting to us from both the seen and the unseen side of life, forces and conditions most akin to those of our own thoughts.

This law is continually operating whether we are conscious of it or not. We are all living, so to speak, in a vast ocean of thought, and the very atmosphere around us is continually filled with the thought forces that are being continually sent or that are continually going out in the form of thought waves. We are all affected, more or less, by these thought forces, either consciously or unconsciously; and in the degree that we are more or less sensitively organized, or in the degree that we are negative and so are open to outside influences, rather than positive, thus determining what influences shall enter into our realm of thought, and hence into our lives.—*In Tune with the Infinite*

The Anchor Of The Sensitively Organized

There are those among us who are much more sensitively organized than others. As an organism their bodies are more finely, more sensitively constructed. These, generally speaking, are people who are always more or less affected by the mentalities of those with whom they come in contact, or in whose company they are. A friend, the editor of one of our great journals, is so sensitively organized that it is impossible for him to attend a gathering, such as a reception, talk and shake hands with a number of people during the course of the evening, without taking on to a greater or less extent their various mental and physical conditions. These affect him to such an extent that he is scarcely himself and in his best condition for work until some two or three days afterward.

Some think it unfortunate for one to be sensitively organized. By no means. It is a good thing, for one may thus be more open and receptive to the higher impulses of the soul within, and to all higher forces and influences from without. It may, however, be unfortunate and extremely inconvenient to be so organized unless one recognize and gain the power of closing himself, of making himself positive to all detrimental or undesirable influences. This power everyone, however sensitively organized he may be, can acquire.

This he can acquire through the mind's action. And, moreover, there is no habit of more value to anyone, be he sensitively or less sensitively organized, than that of occasionally taking and holding himself continually in the attitude of mind — I close myself, I make myself positive to all things below, and open and receptive to all higher influences, to all things above. By taking this attitude of mind consciously now and then, it soon becomes a habit, and if one is deeply in earnest in regard to it, it puts into operation silent but subtle and powerful influences in effecting the desired results. In this way all lower and undesirable influences from both the seen and the unseen side of life are closed out, while all higher influences are invited, and in the degree that they are invited will they enter.

The fact of life in whatever form, means the continuance of life, even though the form be changed. Life is the one eternal principle of the universe and so always continues, even though the form of the agency through which it manifests be changed. "In my Father's house are many mansions." And surely, because the individual has dropped, has gone out of the physical body, there is no evidence at all that the life does not go right on the same as before, not commencing, — for there is no cessation, — but commencing in the other form, exactly where it has left off here; for all life is a continuous evolution, step by step; there one neither skips nor jumps.

We cannot rationally believe other than that those who have laboured in love and with uplifting power here are still labouring in the same way, and in all probability with more earnest zeal, and with still greater power.

"And Elisha prayed, and said, Lord, I pray thee, open his eyes, that he may see. And the Lord opened the eyes of the young man; and he saw: and, behold, the mountain was full of horses and chariots of fire round about Elisha."—*In Tune with the Infinite*

How We Attract Success Or Failure

As science is so abundantly demonstrating today, — the things that we see are but a very small fraction of the things that are. The real, vital forces at work in our own lives and in the world about us are not seen by the ordinary physical eye. Yet they are the causes of which all things we see are merely the effects. Thoughts are forces; like builds like, and like attracts like. For one to govern his thinking, then, is to determine his life.

Says one of deep insight into the nature of things: "The law of correspondences between spiritual and material things is wonderfully exact in its workings. People ruled by the mood of gloom attract to them gloomy things. People always discouraged and despondent do not succeed in anything, and live only by burdening someone else. The hopeful, confident, and cheerful attract the elements of success. A man's front or back yard will advertise that man's ruling mood in the way it is kept.

A woman at home shows her state of mind in her dress. A slattern advertises the ruling mood of hopelessness, carelessness, and lack of system. Rags, tatters, and dirt are always in the mind before being on the body. The thought that is most put out brings its corresponding visible element to crystallize about you as surely and literally as the visible bit of copper in solution attracts to it the invisible copper in that solution. A mind always hopeful, confident, courageous, and determined on its set purpose, and keeping itself to that purpose, attracts to itself out of the elements things and powers favorable to that purpose.

"Every thought of yours has a literal value to you in every possible way. The strength of your body, the strength of your mind, your success in business, and the pleasure your company brings others, depends on the nature of your thoughts. ...In whatever mood you set your mind does your spirit receive of unseen substance in correspondence with that mood. It is as much a chemical law as a spiritual law. Chemistry is not confined to the elements we see. The elements we do not see with the physical eye outnumber ten thousand times those we do see."

Faith is nothing more nor less than the operation of the thought-forces in the form of an earnest desire, coupled with expectation as to its fulfillment. And in the degree that faith, the earnest desire thus sent out, is continually held to and watered by firm expectation, in just that degree does it either draw to itself, or does it change from the unseen into the visible, from the spiritual into the material, that for which it is sent.—*In Tune with the Infinite*

Fear Brings Failure

Nothing is more subtle than thought, nothing more powerful, nothing more irresistible in its operations, when rightly applied and held to with a faith and fidelity that is unswerving, — a faith and fidelity that never knows the neutralizing effects of doubt and fear. If one have aspirations and a sincere desire for a higher and better condition, so far as advantages, facilities, associates, or any surroundings or environments are concerned, and if he continually send out his highest thought forces for the realization of these desires, and continually water these forces with firm expectation as to their fulfillment, he will sooner or later find himself in the realization of these desires, and all in accordance with natural laws and forces.

Fear brings its own fulfillment the same as hope. The same law operates, and if, as our good and valued friend, Job, said when the darkest days were setting in upon him, "That which I feared has come upon me," — was true, how much more surely could he have brought about the opposite conditions, those he would have desired, had he had even the slightest realization of his own powers, and had he acted the part of the master instead of that of the servant; had he dictated terms instead of being dictated to, and thus suffering the consequences.

If one finds himself in any particular condition, in the midst of any surroundings or environments that are not desirable, that have nothing — at least for any length of time — that is of value to him, for his highest life and unfoldment, he has the remedy entirely within his own grasp the moment he realizes the power and supremacy of the forces of the mind and spirit; and, unless he intelligently use these forces, he drifts. Unless through them he becomes master and dictates, he becomes the slave and is dictated to, and so is driven hither and thither.

Earnest, sincere desire, sincere aspiration for higher and better conditions or means to realize them, the thought-forces actively sent out for their realization, these continually watered by firm expectation without allowing the contrary, neutralizing force of fear ever to enter in, —this, accompanied by rightly directed work and activity, will bring about the fullest realization of one's highest desires and aspirations with a certainty as absolute as that effect follows cause. Each and every one of us can thus make for himself ever higher and higher conditions, can attract ever higher and higher influences, can realize an ever higher and higher ideal in life. These are the forces that are within us, simply waiting to be recognized and used, — the forces that we should infuse into and mould everyday life with. The moment we vitally recognize them, they become our servants and wait upon our bidding.

We are born to be neither slaves nor beggars, but to dominion and to plenty. This is our rightful heritage, if we will but recognize and lay claim to it. Many a man and many a woman is today longing for conditions better and higher than he or she is in, who might be using the same time now spent in vain, indefinite, spasmodic longings, in putting into operation forces which, accompanied by the right personal activity, would speedily bring the fullest realization of his or her fondest dreams.—*In Tune with the Infinite*

Heart Training Through The Animal World

It is an established fact that the training of the intellect alone is not sufficient. Nothing in this world can be truer than that the education of the head, without the training of the heart, simply increases one's power for evil, while the education of the heart, along with the head, increases one's power for good, and this, indeed, is the true education.

Clearly we must begin with the child. The lessons learned in childhood are the last to be forgotten. Let them be taught that the lower animals are God's creatures, as they themselves are, put here by a common Heavenly Father, each for its own special purpose, and that they have the same right to life and protection. Let them be taught that principle recognised by all noble-hearted men, that it is only a depraved, debased, and cowardly nature that will injure an inferior, defenceless creature, simply because it is in its power to do so, and that there is no better, no grander test of true bravery and nobility of character than one's treatment of the lower animals.

I cannot refrain in this connection from quoting a sentence or two from Archdeacon Farrar which have recently come to my notice:

"Not once or twice only, at the seaside, have I come across a sad and disgraceful sight — a sight which haunts me still — a number of harmless sea-birds lying defaced and dead upon the sand, their white plumage red with blood, as they had been tossed there, dead or half-dead, their torture and massacre having furnished a day's amusement to heartless and senseless men. Amusement! I say execrable amusement! All killing for mere killing's sake is execrable amusement. Can you imagine the stupid callousness, the utter insensibility to mercy and beauty, of the man who, seeing those bright, beautiful creatures as their white, immaculate wings flash in the sunshine over the blue waves, can go out in a boat with his boys to teach them to become brutes in character by finding amusement — I say, again, dis-humanising amusement — by wantonly murdering these fair birds of God, or cruelly wounding them, and letting them fly away to wait and die in lonely places?"

And another paragraph which was sent me by a kind friend to our fellow-creatures a few days ago : "The celebrated Russian novelist, Turgenieff, tells a most touching incident from his own life, which awakened in him sentiments that have coloured all his writings with a deep and tender feeling.

"When Turgenieff was a boy of ten his father took him out one day bird-shooting. As they tramped across the brown stubble, a golden pheasant rose with a low whirr from the ground at his feet, and, with the joy of a sportsman throbbing through his veins, he raised his gun and fired, wild with excitement when the creature fell fluttering at his side. Life was ebbing fast, but the instinct of the mother was stronger than death itself, and with a feeble flutter of her wings the mother bird reached the nest where her young brood were huddled, unconscious of danger. Then, with such a look of pleading and reproach that his heart stood still at the ruin he had wrought, — and never to his dying day did he forget the feeling of cruelty and guilt that came to him in that moment, — the little brown head toppled over, and only the dead body of the mother shielded her nestlings.

"'Father, father,' he cried, 'what have I done?' as he turned his horror-stricken face to his father. But not to his father's eye had this little tragedy been enacted, and he said: 'Well done, my son; that was well done for your first shot. You will soon be a fine sportsman.'

"'Never, father; never again shall I destroy any living creature. If that is sport I will have none of it. Life is more beautiful to me than death, and since I cannot give life, I will not take it.' "

And so, instead of putting into the hands of the child a gun or any other weapon that may be instrumental in crippling, torturing, or taking the life of even a single animal, I would give him the field-glass and the camera, and send him out to be a friend to the animals, to observe and study their characteristics, their habits, to learn from them those wonderful lessons that can be learned, and thus have his whole nature expand in admiration and love and care for them, and become thereby the truly manly and princely type of man, rather than the careless, callous, brutal type.—*Every Living Creature*

The Secret And The Power Of Love

When we fully realize the great fact of the oneness of all life, — that all are partakers from this one Infinite Source, and so that the same life is the life in each individual, then prejudices go and hatreds cease. Love grows and reigns supreme. Then, wherever we go, whenever we come in contact with the fellowman, we are able to recognize the God within. We thus look only for the good, and we find it. It always pays.

There is a deep scientific fact underlying the great truth, " He that takes the sword shall perish by the sword." The moment we come into a realization of the subtle power of the thought-forces, we can quickly see that the moment we entertain any thoughts of hatred toward another, he gets the effects of these diabolical forces that go out from us, and has the same thoughts of hatred aroused in him, which in turn return to the sender. Then when we understand the effects of the passion, hatred or anger, even upon the physical body, we can see how detrimental, how expensive this is. The same is true in regard to all kindred thoughts or passions, envy, criticism, jealousy, scorn. In the ultimate we shall find that in entertaining feelings of this nature toward another, we always suffer far more than the one toward whom we entertain them.

And then when we fully realize the fact that selfishness is at the root of all error, sin, and crime, and that ignorance is the basis of all selfishness, with what charity we come to look upon the acts of all. It is the ignorant man who seeks his own ends at the expense of the greater whole. It is the ignorant man, therefore, who is the selfish man. The truly wise man is never selfish. He is a seer, and recognizes the fact that he, a single member of the one great body, is benefited in just the degree that the entire body is benefited, and so he seeks nothing for himself that he would not equally seek for all mankind.

If selfishness is at the bottom of all error, sin, and crime, and ignorance is the basis of all selfishness, then when we see a manifestation of either of these qualities, if we are true to the highest within us, we will look for and will seek to call forth the good in each individual with whom we come in contact. When God speaks to God, then God responds, and shows forth as God. But when devil speaks to devil, then devil responds, and the devil is always to pay.

I sometimes hear a person say, " I don't see any good in him." No! Then you are no seer. Look deeper and you will find the very God in every human soul. But remember it takes a God to recognize a God. Christ always spoke to the highest, the truest, and the best in men. He knew and he recognized the God in each because He had first realized it in Himself. He ate with publicans and sinners. Abominable, the Scribes and Pharisees said. They were so wrapped up in their own conceits, their own self-centeredness, hence their own ignorance, that they had never found the God in themselves, and so they never dreamed that it was the real life of even publicans and sinners.

In the degree that we hold a person in the thought of evil or of error, do we suggest evil and error to him. In the degree that he is sensitively organized, or not well individualized, and so, subject to the suggestions of the thought-forces from others, will he be influenced; and so in this way we may be sharers in the very evildoing in which we hold another in thought. In the same way when we hold a person in the thought of the right, the good, and the true, righteousness, goodness, and truth are suggested to him, and thus we have a most beneficent influence on his life and conduct. If our hearts go out in love to all with whom we come in contact, we inspire love, and the same ennobling and warming influences of love always return to us from those in whom we inspire them. There is a deep scientific principle underlying the precept — If you would have all the world love you, you must first love all the world.

In the degree that we love will we be loved. Thoughts are forces. Each creates of its kind. Each comes back laden with the effect that corresponds to itself and of which it is the cause.

"Then let your secret thoughts be fair — They have a vital part, and share in shaping words and moulding fate; God's system is so intricate."

I know of no better practice than that of a friend who continually holds himself in an attitude of mind that he continually sends out his love in the form of the thought, — "Dear everybody, I love you." And when we realize the fact that a thought invariably produces its effect before it returns, or before it ceases, we can see how he is continually breathing out a blessing not only upon all with whom he comes in contact, but upon all the world. These same thoughts of love, moreover, tokened in various ways, are continually coming to him from all quarters.—*In Tune with the Infinite*

Then Give To The World The Best You Have, And The Best Will Come Back To You

What a privilege and how enjoyable it would be to live and walk in a world where we meet only Gods. In such a world you can live. In such a world I can live. For in the degree that we come into this higher realization do we see only the God in each human soul; and when we are thus able to see him in everyone we meet, we then live in such a world

And when we thus recognize the God in everyone, we by this recognition help to call it forth ever more and more. What a privilege — this privilege of yours, this privilege of mine! That hypocritical judging of another is something then with which we can have nothing to do; for we have the power of looking beyond the evolving, changing, error-making self, and seeing the real, the changeless, the eternal self which by and by will show forth in the full beauty of holiness. We are then large enough also to realize the fact that when we condemn another, by that very act we condemn ourselves

This realization so fills us with love that we continually overflow it, and all with whom we come in contact feel its warming and life-giving power. These in turn send back the same feelings of love to us, and so we continually attract love from all quarters. Tell me how much one loves and I will tell you how much he has seen of God. Tell me how much he loves and I will tell you how much he lives with God. Tell me how much he loves and I will tell you how far into the Kingdom of Heaven, — the kingdom of harmony, he has entered, for "love is the fulfilling of the law."

And in a sense love is everything. It is the key to life, and its influences are those that move the world. Live only in the thought of love for all and you will draw love to you from all. Live in the thought of malice or hatred, and malice and hatred will come back to you.

"For evil poisons; malice shafts like boomerangs return, inflicting wounds that will not heal while rage and anger burn."

Every thought you entertain is a force that goes out, and every thought comes back laden with its kind. This is an immutable law. Every thought you entertain has moreover a direct effect upon your body. Love and its kindred emotions are the normal and the natural, those in accordance with the eternal order of the universe, for "God is love." These have a life-giving, health-engendering influence upon your body, besides beautifying your countenance, enriching your voice, and making you ever more attractive in every way. And as it is true that in the degree that you hold thoughts of love for all, you call the same from them in return, and as these have a direct effect upon your mind, and through your mind upon your body, it is as so much life force added to your own from without. You are then continually building this into both your mental and your physical life, and so your life is enriched by its influence.

Hatred and all its kindred emotions are the unnatural, the abnormal, the perversions, and so, out of harmony with the eternal order of the universe. For if love is the fulfilling of the law, then these, its opposites, are direct violations of law, and there can never be a violation of law without its attendant pain and suffering in one form or another. There is no escape from this. And what is the result of this particular form of violation? When you allow thoughts of anger, hatred, malice, jealousy, envy, criticism, or scorn to exercise sway, they have a corroding and poisoning effect upon the organism; they pull it down, and if allowed to continue will eventually tear it to pieces by externalizing themselves in the particular forms of disease they give rise to. And then in addition to the destructive influences from your own mind you are continually calling the same influences from other minds, and these come as destructive forces augmenting your own, thus aiding in the tearing-down process.

And so love inspires love; hatred breeds hatred. Love and good-will stimulate and build up the body; hatred and malice corrode and tear it down. Love is a savor of life unto life; hatred is a savor of death unto death.

"There are loyal hearts, there are spirits brave, There are souls that are pure and true; Then give to the world the best you have. And the best will come back to you.

"Give love, and love to your heart will flow. A strength in your utmost need; Have faith, and a score of hearts will show their faith in your word and deed."—*In Tune with the Infinite*

Hatred Never Ceases By Hatred, But By Love

Love is positive, and stronger than hatred. Hatred can always be conquered by love. On the other hand, if you meet hatred with hatred, you simply intensify it. You add fuel to the flame already kindled, upon which it will feed and grow, and so you increase and intensify the evil conditions. Nothing is to be gained by it, everything is to be lost. By sending love for hatred you will be able to so neutralize it that it will not only have no effect upon you, but will not be able even to reach you. But more than this, you will by this course sooner or later be able literally to transmute the enemy into the friend. Meet hatred with hatred and you degrade yourself. Meet hatred with love and you elevate not only yourself but also the one who bears you hatred.

The Persian sage has said, "Always meet petulance with gentleness, and perverseness with kindness. A gentle hand can lead even an elephant by a hair. Reply to thine enemy with gentleness. Opposition to peace is sin." The Buddhist says, "If a man foolishly does me wrong I will return him the protection of my ungrudging love. The more evil comes from him, the more good shall go from me." "The wise man avenges injuries by benefits," says the Chinese. "Return good for evil, overcome anger by love; hatred never ceases by hatred, but by love," says the Hindu.

The truly wise man or woman will recognize no one as an enemy. Occasionally we hear the expression, "Never mind; I'll get even with him." Will you? And how will you do it? You can do it in one of two ways. You can, as you have in mind, deal with him as he deals, or apparently deals, with you, — pay him, as we say, in his own coin. If you do this you will get even with him by sinking yourself to his level, and both of you will suffer by it. Or, you can show yourself the larger, you can send him love for hatred, kindness for ill-treatment, and so get even with him by raising him to the higher level. But remember that you can never help another without by that very act helping yourself; and if forgetful of self, then in most all cases the value to you is greater than the service you render another. If you are ready to treat him as he treats you, then you show clearly that there is in you that which draws the hatred and ill-treatment to you; you deserve what you are getting and should not complain, nor would you complain if you were wise. By following the other course you most effectually accomplish your purpose, — you gain a victory for yourself, and at the same time you do a great service for him, of which it is evident he stands greatly in need.

Thus you may become his saviour. He in turn may become the saviour of other error-making, and consequently care-encumbered men and women. Many times the struggles are greater than we can ever know. We need more gentleness and sympathy and compassion in our common human life. Then we will neither blame nor condemn. Instead of blaming or condemning we will sympathize, and all the more we will:

"Comfort one another, for the way is often dreary, and the feet are often weary, and the heart is very sad. There is a heavy burden bearing, when it seems that none are caring, and we half forget that ever we were glad.

"Comfort one another with the hand-clasp close and tender. With the sweetness love can render, and the looks of friendly eyes. Do not wait with grace unspoken while life's daily bread is broken — Gentle speech is oft like manna from the skies."—*In Tune with the Infinite*

Thought And Its Intelligent Direction

Of all known forms of energy, thought is the most subtle, the most irresistible force. It has always been operating; but, so far as the great masses of the people are concerned, it has been operating blindly, or, rather, they have been blind to its mighty power, except in the cases of a few here and there. And these, as a consequence, have been our prophets, our seers, our sages, our saviours, our men of great and mighty power. We are just beginning to grasp the tremendous truth that there is a science of thought, and that the laws governing it can be known and scientifically applied.

Thought needs direction to be effective, and upon this effective results depend as much as upon the force itself. This brings us to the will. Will is not, as is so often thought, a force in itself; will is the directing power. Thought is the force. Will gives direction. Thought scattered gives the weak, the uncertain, the vacillating, the aspiring, but the never-doing, the I-would-like-to, but the get-no-where, the attain-to-nothing man or woman.

Thought steadily directed by the will gives the strong, the firm, the never-yielding; the never-know-defeat man or woman, the man or woman who uses the very difficulties and hindrances that would dishearten the ordinary person, as stones with which he paves a way over which he triumphantly walks, who, by the very force he carries with him, so neutralizes and transmutes the very obstacles that would bar his way that they fall before him, and in turn aid him on his way; the man or, woman who, like the eagle, uses the very contrary wind that would thwart his flight, that would turn him and carry him in the opposite direction, as the very agency upon which he mounts and mounts and mounts, until actually lost to the human eye, and which, in addition to thus aiding him, brings to him an ever fuller realization of his own powers, or in other words, an ever greater power.

It is this that gives the man or the woman who in storm or in sunny weather, rides over every obstacle, throws before him every barrier, and, as Browning has said, finally "arrives." Take, for example, the successful business man, —for it is all one, the law is the same in all cases — the man who started with nothing except his own interior equipments. He has made up his mind to one thing, — success. This is his ideal. He thinks success, he sees success. He refuses to see anything else. He expects success: he thus attracts it to him, his thought-forces continually attract to him every agency that makes for success. He has set up the current, so that every wind that blows brings him success. He doesn't expect failure, and so he doesn't invite it. He has no time, no energies, to waste in fears or forebodings. He is dauntless, untiring, in his efforts. Let disaster come today, and tomorrow — ay, even yet today — he is getting his bearings, he is setting forces anew into operation; and these very forces are of more value to him than the half million dollars of his neighbor who has suffered from the same disaster.

We speak of a man's failing in business, little thinking that the real failure came long before, and that the final crash is but the culmination, the outward visible manifestation, of the real failure that occurred within possibly long ago. A man carries his success or his failure with him: it is not dependent upon outside conditions.—*In Tune with the Infinite*

Will — The Human And The Divine

Will is the steady directing power: it is concentration. It is the pilot which, after the vessel is started by the mighty force within, puts it on its right course and keeps it true to that course.

Will is the magnifying glass which so concentrates and so focuses the sun's rays that they quickly burn a hole through the paper that is held before it. The same rays, not thus concentrated, not thus focused, would fall upon the paper for days without any effect whatever. Will is the means for the directing, the concentrating, the focusing, of the thought-forces. Thought under wise direction, — this it is that does the work, that brings results, that makes the successful career. One object in mind which we never lose sight of; an ideal steadily held before the mind, never lost sight of, never lowered, never swerved from, — this, with persistence, determines all. Nothing can resist the power of thought, when thus directed by will.

May not this power, then, be used for base as well as for good purposes, for selfish as well as for unselfish ends? The same with this modification, — the more highly thought is spiritualized, the more subtle and powerful it becomes; and the more highly spiritualized the life, the farther is it removed from base, ignoble, selfish ends. But, even if it can be thus used, let him who would so use it be careful, let him never forget that that mighty, searching, omnipotent law of the right, of truth, of justice, that runs through all the universe and that can never be annulled or even for a moment set aside, will drive him to the wall, will crush him with a terrific force if he so use it. Let him never forget that whatever he may get for self at the expense of someone else, through deception, through misrepresentation, through the exercise of the lower functions and powers, will by a law equally subtle, equally powerful, be turned into ashes in his very hands.

The honey he thinks he has secured will be turned into bitterness as he attempts to eat it; the beautiful fruit he thinks is his will be as wormwood as he tries to enjoy it; the rose he has plucked will vanish, and he will find himself clutching a handful of thorns, which will penetrate to the very quick and which will

flow the very life-blood from his hands. For through the violation
of a higher, an immutable law, though he may get this or that, the
power of true enjoyment will be taken away, and what he gets will
become as a thorn in his side: either this or it will sooner or later
escape from his hands. God's triumphal car moves in a direction
and at a rate that is certain and absolute, and he who would
oppose it or go contrary to it must fall and be crushed beneath its
wheels; and for him this crushing is necessary, in order that it may
bring him the more quickly to a knowledge of the higher laws, to
a realization of the higher self.

This brings to our notice two orders of will, which we may term,
for convenience' sake, the human and the divine. The human will
is the one just noticed, the sense will, the will of the lower self,
that which seeks its own ends regardless of its connection with the
greater whole. The divine will is the will of the higher self, the
God-self, that never makes an error, that never leads into
difficulties.

It is thus that the Infinite Power works through and for us —
true inspiration — while our part is simply to see that our
connection with this power is consciously and perfectly kept.—*In
Tune with the Infinite*

The Secret Of The Highest Power

The secret of the highest power is simply the uniting of the outer agencies of expression with the Power that works from within.

Are you a painter? Then in the degree that you open yourself to the power of the forces within will you become great instead of mediocre. You can never put into permanent form inspirations higher than those that come through your own soul. In order for the higher inspirations to come through it, you must open your soul, you must open it fully to the Supreme Source of all inspiration. Are you an orator? In the degree that you come into harmony and work in conjunction with the higher powers that will speak through you will you have the real power of moulding and of moving men. If you use merely your physical agents, you will be simply a demagogue. If you open yourself so that the voice of God can speak through and use your physical agents, you will become a great and true orator, great and true in just the degree that you so open yourself.

Are you a singer? Then open yourself and let the God within pour forth in the spirit of song. You will find it a thousand times easier than all your long and studied practice without this, and other things being equal, there will come to you a power of song so enchanting and so enrapturing that its influence upon all who hear will be irresistible.

When my cabin or tent has been pitched during the summer on the edge or in the midst of a forest, I have sometimes lain awake on my cot in the early morning, just as the day was beginning to break. Silence at first. Then an intermittent chirp here and there. And as the unfolding tints of the dawn became faintly perceptible, these grew more and more frequent, until by and by the whole forest seemed to burst forth in one grand chorus of song. Wonderful! wonderful! It seemed as if the very trees, as if every grass-blade, as if the bushes, the very sky above, and the earth beneath, had part in this wonderful symphony. Then, as I have listened as it went on and on, I have thought, What a study in the matter of song! If we could but learn from the birds. If we could but open ourselves to the same powers and allow them to pour forth in us, what singers, what movers of men we might have! Nay, what singers and what movers of men we would have!

When we open ourselves to the highest inspirations they never fail us. When we fail to do this we fail in attaining the highest results, whatever the undertaking.

Are you a writer? Then remember that the one great precept underlying all successful literary work is, Look into thine own heart and write. Be true. Be fearless. Be loyal to the promptings of your own soul. Remember that an author can never write more than he himself is. If he would write more, then he must be more. He is simply his own amanuensis. He in a sense writes himself into his book. He can put no more into it than he himself is.

If he is one of a great personality, strong in purpose, deep in feeling, open always to the highest inspirations, a certain indefinable something gets into his pages that makes them breathe forth a vital, living power, a power so great that each reader gets the same inspirations as those that spoke through the author. That that's written between the lines is many times more than that that's written in the lines. It is the spirit of the author that engenders this power.

The one, on the other hand, who fears to depart from beaten paths, who allows himself to be bound by arbitrary rules, limits his own creative powers in just the degree that he allows himself so to be bound. "My book," says one of the greatest of modern authors," shall smell of the pines and resound with the hum of insects. The swallow over my window shall interweave that thread or straw he carries in his bill into my web also." Far better, gentle sage, to have it smell of the pines and resound with the hum of insects than to have it sound of the rules that a smaller type of man gets by studying the works of a few great, fearless writers like yourself, and formulating from what he thus gains a handbook of rhetoric. "Of no use are the men who study to do exactly as was done before, who can never understand that today is a new day."—*In Tune with the Infinite*

Wisdom: Or Interior Illumination

In order for the highest wisdom and insight we must have absolute confidence in the Divine guiding us, but not through the channel of someone else. And why should we go to another for knowledge and wisdom? With God is no respect of persons. Why should we seek these things secondhand? Why should we thus stultify our own innate powers? Why should we not go direct to the Infinite Source itself? "If any man lack wisdom let him ask of God." " Before they call I will answer, and while they are yet speaking, I will hear."

When we thus go directly to the Infinite Source itself we are no longer slaves to personalities, institutions, or books. We should always keep ourselves open to suggestions of truth from these agencies. We should always regard them as agencies, however, and never as sources. We should never recognize them as masters, but simply as teachers. With Browning, we must recognize the great fact that :

"Truth is within ourselves; it takes no rise from outward things, whate'er you may believe. There is an inmost centre in us all, where truth abides in fullness."

There is no more important injunction in all the world, nor one with a deeper interior meaning, than "To thine own self be true." In other words, be true to your own soul, for it is through your own soul that the voice of God speaks to you. This is the interior guide. This is "the light that lighteth every man that cometh into the world." This is conscience. This is intuition. This is the voice of the higher self, the voice of the soul, the voice of God. "Thou shalt hear a voice behind thee, saying: This is the way, walk ye in it."

When Elijah was on the mountain it was after the various physical commotions and manifestations that he heard the "still, small voice," the voice of his own soul, through which the Infinite God was speaking. If we will but follow this voice of intuition, it will speak ever more clearly and more plainly, until by and by it will be absolute and unerring in its guidance. The great trouble with us is that we do not listen to and do not follow this voice within our own souls, and so we become as a house divided against itself. We are pulled this way and that, and we are never certain of anything. I have a friend who listens so carefully to this inner voice, who, in other words, always acts so quickly and so fully in accordance with his intuitions, and whose life as a consequence is so absolutely guided by them, that he always does the right thing at the right time and in the right way. He always knows when to act and how to act, and he is never in the condition of a house divided against itself.

But someone says, "May it not be dangerous for us to act always upon our intuitions? Suppose we should have an intuition to do harm to someone?" We need not be afraid of this, however, for the voice of the soul, this voice of God speaking through the soul, will never direct one to do harm to another, nor to do anything that is not in accordance with the highest: standards of right, and truth, and justice. And if you at any time have a prompting of this kind, know that it is not the voice of intuition; it is some characteristic of your lower self that is prompting you.

Reason is not to be set aside, but it is to be continually illumined by this higher spiritual perception, and in the degree that it is thus illumined will it become an agent of light and power. When one becomes thoroughly individualized he enters into the realm of all knowledge and wisdom; and to be individualized is to recognize no power outside of the Infinite Power that is back of all. When one recognizes this great fact and opens himself to this Spirit of Infinite Wisdom, he then enters upon the road to the true education, and mysteries that before were closed now reveal themselves to him. This must indeed be the foundation of all true education, this evolving from within, this evolving of what has been involved by the Infinite Power.

There are no new stars, there are no new laws or forces, but we can so open ourselves to this Spirit of Infinite Wisdom that we can discover and recognize those that have not been known before; and in this way they become new to us.

"This is true wisdom. Wisdom is the knowledge of God." Wisdom comes by intuition. It far transcends knowledge. Great knowledge, knowledge of many things, may be had by virtue simply of a very retentive memory. It comes by tuition. But wisdom far transcends knowledge, in that knowledge is a mere incident of this deeper wisdom.—*In Tune with the Infinite*

Let There Be Many Windows In Your Soul

He who would enter into the realm of wisdom must first divest himself of all intellectual pride. He must become as a little child. Prejudices, preconceived opinions, and beliefs always stand in the way of true wisdom. Conceited opinions are always suicidal in their influences. They bar the door to the entrance of truth.

All about us we see men in the religious world, in the world of science, in the political, in the social world, who through intellectual pride are so wrapped in their own conceits and prejudices that larger and later revelations of truth can find no entrance to them; and instead of growing and expanding, they are becoming dwarfed and stunted, and still more incapable of receiving truth. Instead of actively aiding in the progress of the world, they are as so many dead sticks in the way that would retard the wheels of progress. This, however, they can never do. Such always in time get bruised, broken, and left behind, while God's triumphal car of truth moves steadily onward.

When the steam engine was still being experimented with, and before it was perfected sufficiently to come into practical use, a well-known Englishman —well known then in scientific circles —wrote an extended pamphlet proving that it would be impossible for it ever to be used in ocean navigation, that is, in a trip involving the crossing of the ocean, because it would be utterly impossible for any vessel to carry with it sufficient coal for the use of its furnace. And the interesting feature of the whole matter was that the very first steam vessel that made the trip from England to America, had among its cargo a part of the first edition of this carefully prepared pamphlet. There was only the one edition. Many editions might be sold now. This seems indeed an amusing fact; but far more amusing is the man who voluntarily closes himself to truth because, forsooth, it does not come through conventional, or orthodox, or heretofore accepted channels; or because it may not be in full accord with, or possibly may be opposed to, established usages or beliefs. On the contrary :—

"Let there be many windows in your soul, that all the glory of the universe may beautify it. Not the narrow pane of one poor creed can catch the radiant rays that shine from countless sources.

Tear away the blinds of superstition: let the light pour through fair windows, broad as truth itself, and high as heaven. . . . Tune your ear to all the wordless music of the stars and to the voice of Nature, and your heart shall turn to truth and goodness as the plant turns to the sun. A thousand unseen hands reach down to help you to their peace-crowned heights, and all the forces of the firmament shall fortify your strength. Be not afraid to thrust aside half-truths and grasp the whole."

There is a great law in connection with the coming of truth. It is this: Whenever a man or a woman shuts himself or herself to the entrance of truth on account of intellectual pride, preconceived opinions, prejudices, or for whatever reason, there is a great law which says that truth in its fullness will come to that one from no source. And on the other hand, when a man or a woman opens himself or herself fully to the entrance of truth from whatever source it may come, there is an equally great law which says that truth will flow in to him or to her from all sources, from all quarters. Such becomes the free man, the free woman, for it is the truth that makes us free. The other remains in bondage, for truth has had no invitation and will not enter where it is not fully and freely welcomed.

And where truth is denied entrance the rich blessings it carries with it cannot take up their abode. On the contrary, when this is the case, it sends an envoy carrying with it atrophy, disease, death, physically and spiritually as well as intellectually. And the man who would rob another of his free and unfettered search for truth, who would stand as the interpreter of truth for another, with the intent of remaining in this position, rather than endeavoring to lead him to the place where he can be his own interpreter, is more to be shunned than a thief and a robber. The injury he works is far greater, for he is doing direct and positive injury to the very life of the one he thus holds.

Who has ever appointed any man, whoever he may be, as the keeper, the custodian, the dispenser of God's illimitable truth? Many indeed are moved and so are called to be teachers of truth; but the true teacher will never stand as the interpreter of truth for another. The true teacher is the one whose endeavor is to bring the one he teaches to a true knowledge of himself and hence of his own interior powers, that he may become his own interpreter. All others are, generally speaking, those animated by purely personal motives, self-aggrandizement, or personal gain. Moreover, he who would claim to have all truth and the only truth, is a bigot, a fool, or a knave.—*In Tune with the Infinite*

As To The Quality Of Our Education

Every child in school until a certain age or until a sufficient equipment to meet the ordinary duties of life is reached, should be the nation's motto.

It is also eminently fitting that something be said of the quality of the education it is proposed to make compulsory attendance upon universal. To come at once to the point in mind and briefly — training of the intellect alone is not sufficient; we shall remain a long way off from the ideal until we make moral, humane, heart-training a far more important feature of our educational systems than we have made it thus far. We are advancing in this respect, but we have great advances yet to make. Kindness and consideration, sympathy and fraternity, love of justice — the full and ready willingness to give it as well as to demand it, the clearcut comprehension of the majesty and beauty that escapes into the life of the individual as he understands and appropriates to himself the all-embracing contents of the golden rule.

The training of the intellect alone at the expense of the "humanities " has made or has enlarged the power of many a criminal, many a usurper of other men's homes and property, many an oppressor, and has thereby added poison and desolation to his own life as well as to the lives of those with whom he has come in contact and who have felt his blighting and withering influence. It is also chiefly from those without this training, that that great body of our fellow-creatures which we term the animal world, receive their most thoughtless and cruel treatment, and perhaps from· among none more than among the rich and fashionable.

I think there is another feature in our educational systems that we would do wisely to give more attention to. In a nation of free institutions, more attention could wisely be given to systematic and concrete instruction in connection with the institutions of government, and in connection with this a training in civic pride that sees to it that our public offices are filled with men of at least ordinary honesty and integrity, men who regard public office as a public trust worthy the service of their highest manhood, rather than with those whose eye is single to the largest amount of loot and graft that comes within the range of their vision and the reach of their hand.

Such a system would in time spell the end of Tammany Hall —a Democratic organization in New York City, whose chief object is to make politics a cover to divert the largest possible sums of money from the people of the City of New York to line the pockets, and in great abundance, of those in control of the body of loot. It would in time spell the end of the Republican rings and halls whose object and purpose is identically the same in every city where they have been able to gain control, as well as the Democratic rings in cities other than New York. The methods of the rings of the one are equally black with the methods of the rings of the other; where the motives are the same the resultant action is the same.

Our educational methods are developing. In educational work are some of our noblest, our foremost men and women. There is an element of the practical, the useful, that is now sort of remodelling our earlier methods. It has always seemed to me that not only in our public schools but in our colleges and universities, it is possible to get as great a degree of training from branches that are in themselves useful, that will be of actual use later on, as out of those that are used for their training value only. The element of the useful, not at the expense of the training, but combined with it, should be, I think, and is coming to be, the marked feature of our developing educational methods.

The bread and butter problem will be the problem of practically all in our common or public schools today. There probably will not be one in a thousand whose problem it will not be. To make our educational systems so that they will be of the greatest practical aid to all as they enter upon life's activities should, it seems to me, be one of our greatest aims. That our college courses can be improved to at least from twenty to forty per cent along this same line I am fully persuaded, in addition to the saving of considerable valuable time for those who, contemplating professional careers, will afterwards have to spend a considerable period in years in professional schools.

When we consider that not more than one-tenth of one per cent of those in our common schools ever get as far as the college or university, we can see how important it is that every child be guaranteed what the law of the most ordinary justice demands, that he or she have the benefit at least of what will enable him or her to enter upon the stage of young manhood and young womanhood free from the tremendous handicaps with which so many are entering upon it today.—*In the Fire of the Heart*

A New Order Of Patriotism

A new order of patriotism is coming into being and among us. What was at one time confined to the few brave, independent, advanced men, is now becoming common among the people. We are finding that the elements of justice and righteousness, fraternity and godliness, have a very direct relation to, or rather, that patriotism has a very direct relation to them. War — war and the flag, were at one time supposed to be the only agents with which patriotism was linked. To hurrah for the flag and to be eager to go to the front, when the war bugles sounded, or were likely to sound, was for a long period a prevailing idea of patriotism. It may still be a way in which patriotism may be manifested.

The people are learning the real cause of many wars, indeed the great majority of them — the bull-headedness or pig-headedness, the incapacity on the part of those having to do with affairs; and again, the throwing of an entire nation into war by large and powerful though unscrupulous financial interests solely for gain. These two agents are responsible for the great bulk, indeed for nine out of every ten, of all modern wars, even as they have been for all time past. Men are beginning to realize that instead of having anything to do with this type of war, patriotism lies in refusing absolutely to aid or abet it and in using one's influence in a similar way among one's neighbours more blunt and with less power of discernment.

When we reach a point where the large body of citizens see to it that these men and their agents — for the large financial interests of the unscrupulous type almost invariably work through agents many of whom they place or have the people place in public positions — when, I repeat, the larger body of citizens see to it that these men and their agents are kept out of public office and relegate them to the subordinate place where they rightly belong, then we will witness the full birth of an entirely new and a higher order of patriotism that is soon to be dominant among us.

The highest patriotism that I know is that which impels a man to be honest, kind, hence thoughtful in all his business relations and in his daily life; that impels him to the primary and to give attention to those features of our political institutions that are of even greater consequence than his casting his vote on election day; that impels him to think and to be discriminating in his thought; that enables him to be not afraid to point out and denounce the pure self-seeker and his demagogic ways, be he in public life, in the ranks of high standing financiers, or in the ranks of organized labour, or in the ranks of the common life.

It is this patriotism in the common life that is of the high quality. Men who are industrious and honest in their work; who are faithful to whatever tasks are imposed upon them; who are as eager to give justice as to demand it; who are working industriously and intelligently in order to take care of themselves and those dependent upon them, and thus remain self-supporting members of the community; who remain brave and sweet in their natures and who abide always in faith in face of the hard or uncertain times that come at some time or another and in some form or another into the lives of everyone of us; who are jealous of their country's honour, and of the administration of its internal affairs, for in the life of the nation as in the life of the individual, all life is from within out, and as is the inner so always will be the outer. These, I repeat, are the men and these are the conditions that are giving birth to that new and that higher order of patriotism that is now coming among us, and that is to take captive the hearts of men.

That wars in the past have been, and even at the present time are too frequent, all thinking men and women are agreed. That they are in the great majority of cases entirely inexcusable, and that there is and should be very little use for military forces if any, outside of purposes of defence, the highest and most intelligent portion of our citizenship thoroughly believes. And so far as effectiveness is concerned it has been proven time and again, that a citizen soldiery is the finest in the world. Neither vast bodies of men drawn off from creative and productive enterprises and made into a professional soldier class, nor bodies of hirelings, but men who are citizens of intelligence and training, and who stand with the ear ready for the call to arms when there is just cause for their hearing this call, such are the intelligent, such are the brave and the daring, such are the most effective.

Men will not fight effectively for the little price in money they are paid. They will not fight effectively for the glory of another, nor will they fight effectively for a mere tract of land. But where homes are and institutions that they love and revere and care for, then men will fight with all that triumphant intelligence and all that indomitable daring that it is possible to call forth. With a citizen soldiery ready at the just moment to come from the mine, the mill, the counting-house, the farm, thousands of thousands or millions strong, why should there be a vast professional soldiery, a great non-producing class kept primarily for the glory and to do the bidding of a ruling class, but supported almost entirely by the great common people, that is true of the foolhardy military systems of various European countries today?

So far then as the soldiery of a nation is concerned, let the interests of all the people be equally taken care of, let there be institutions founded upon justice, upon equal opportunities for all and special privileges for no man, let there be homes and sentiment encircling these homes, and the keeping up of a large military system becomes but a fool's dream. There will come from such a people a citizen soldiery more intelligent, more brave and determined, and therefore more effective, than can ever come from any professional fighting class, and at a cost not a hundredth part as great.

Take sentiment from the battle-field and you take its chief source of heroism away. The people of homes and of just institutions are a people of sentiment. Upon every cartridge-box and upon every rifle and upon every field piece of such a soldiery the word "Invincible" could most rightly be stamped.—*In the Fire of the Heart*

Men Of Exceptional Executive And Financial Ability

The great nation is, again, the nation in which the man of great natural executive or financial ability finds contentment in a smaller amount of possessions for himself, and the larger contentment and satisfaction and joy in using that unusual ability in the service of, for the benefit of, his city, his state, the nation. The wonder is that more are not doing this already. What an influence a few such men could have, what results they could accomplish, what real riches they could bring into their lives through the riches they would bring into the lives of multitudes — What gratitude would go to them!

As men continue to see the small satisfaction there is in the possession of great ability of this nature, and in the possession of great wealth when divorced from an adequate or even from an abundant connection with the interests and the welfare of their fellow-men, and as they catch the undying truth of the great law of life as enunciated by One who though He had not even where to lay His head was greater than them all — He that is greatest among you shall be your servant — then they in company with all men will be the gainers.

Think what could be accomplished in the nation along the lines we have been considering in this little volume by a company of such men devoted to such ends. A change is coming and very rapidly. The time has already arrived when we will no longer look upon the possession of mere wealth or the ability to get it as deserving of any special distinction, and especially when the means adopted in its acquirement are other than those of absolute honour and rectitude. How significant are the following observations from the "Outlook:"

"Those who have fallen most completely under the spell of fortune-hunting, and have been consumed by the fever of a pursuit which dries up the very sources of spiritual life, can no longer be blind to the fact that when great wealth ceases to be associated with character, honour, genius, or public respect, it is a very shabby substitute for the thing men once held it to be. There are hosts of honourable men of wealth, and there are large fortunes which have been honourably made; but so much brutal indifference to the rights of others, so much tyrannical use of power, so much arbitrary employment of privilege without a touch of genius, so much cynical indifference to human ties of all kinds, so much vulgar greed, have come to light, . . . that the lustre has very largely gone and wealth, as a supreme prize of life, has immensely lost in attractive power. There are hosts of young men who are ambitious to be rich, but who are not willing to accept wealth on such terms; the price is too great, the bargain too hard."

Men of exceptional executive and financial ability, raise yourselves to the standing-point of real greatness and use these abilities to noble purposes and to undying ends instead of piling a heap of things together that you'll soon have to leave and that may do those to whom it will go more harm than good. The times are changing, mankind is advancing and ascending to higher standing places, and it will be but a short time when your position if maintained as at present will be a very ordinary one or even a very low one in the public esteem — and so will be your memories.

The Bishop of Exeter voices a well-nigh universal human cry at present when he says: Give us men!, strong and stalwart ones: men whom highest hope inspires, men whom purest honour fires, men who trample Self beneath them, men who make their country wreathe them As her noble sons, worthy of their sires. Men who never shame their mothers, men who never fail their brothers, true, however false are others: Give us Men — I say again, Give us Men!—*In the Fire of the Heart*

An Example - A Very Young Old Lady

A close observer, a careful student of the power of the thought forces, will soon be able to read in the voice, in the movements, in the features, the effects registered by the prevailing mental states and conditions. Or, if he is told the prevailing mental states and conditions, he can describe the voice, the movements, the features, as well as describe, in a general way, the peculiar physical ailments their possessor is heir to.

There comes to mind at this moment a friend, a lady well on to eighty years of age. An old lady, some, most people in fact, would call her, especially those who measure age by the number of the seasons that have come and gone since one's birth. But to call our friend old, would be to call black white. She is no older than a girl of twenty-five, and indeed younger, I am glad to say, or I am sorry to say, depending upon the point of view, than many a girl of this age. Seeking for the good in all people and in all things, she has found the good everywhere. The brightness of disposition and of voice that is hers today, that attracts all people to her and that makes her so beautifully attractive to all people, has characterized her all through life. It has in turn carried brightness and hope and courage and strength to hundreds and thousands of people through all these years, and will continue to do so, apparently, for many years yet to come.

No fears, no worryings, no hatreds, no jealousies, no sorrowings, no grievings, no sordid graspings after inordinate gain, have found entrance into her realm of thought. As a consequence her mind, free from these abnormal states and conditions, has not externalized in her body the various physical ailments that the great majority of people are lugging about with them, thinking in their ignorance, that they are natural, and that it is all in accordance with the "eternal order of things" that they should have them. Her life has been one of varied experiences, so that all these things would have found ready entrance into the realm of her mind and so into her life were she ignorant enough to allow them entrance. On the contrary she has been wise enough to recognize the fact that in one kingdom at least she is ruler, — the kingdom of her mind, and that it is hers to dictate as to what shall and what shall not enter there. She knows, moreover, that in determining this she is determining all the conditions of her life. It is indeed a pleasure as well as an inspiration to see her as she goes here and there, to see her sunny disposition, her youthful step, to hear her joyous laughter. Indeed and in truth, Shakespeare knew whereof he spoke when he said, — " It is the mind that makes the body rich."

With great pleasure I watched her but recently as she was walking along the street, stopping to have a word and so a part in the lives of a group of children at play by the wayside, hastening her step a little to have a word with a washerwoman toting her bundle of clothes, stopping for a word with a laboring man returning with dinner pail in hand from his work, returning the recognition from the lady in her carriage, and so imparting some of her own rich life to all with whom she came in contact.

And as good fortune would have it, while still watching her, an old lady passed her, — really old, this one, though at least ten or fifteen years younger, so far as the count by the seasons is concerned. Nevertheless she was bent in form and apparently stiff in joint and muscle. Silent in mood, she wore a countenance of long-faced sadness, which was intensified surely several fold by a black, sombre head-gear with an immense heavy veil still more sombre looking if possible. Her entire dress was of this description. By this relic-of-barbarism garb, combined with her own mood and expression, she continually proclaimed to the world two things, — her own personal sorrows and woes, which by this very method she kept continually fresh in her mind, and also her lack of faith in the eternal goodness of things, her lack of faith in the love and eternal goodness of the Infinite Father.

Wrapped only in the thoughts of her own ailments, and sorrows, and woes, she received and she gave nothing of joy, nothing of hope, nothing of courage, nothing of value to those whom she passed or with whom she came in contact. But on the contrary she suggested to all and helped to intensify in many, those mental states all too prevalent in our common human life. And as she passed our friend one could notice a slight turn of the head which, coupled with the expression in her face, seemed to indicate this as her thought, — Your dress and your conduct are not wholly in keeping with a lady of your years. Thank God, then, thank God they are not. And may He in His great goodness and love send us an innumerable company of the same rare type; and may they live a thousand years to bless mankind, to impart the life-giving influences of their own royal lives to the numerous ones all about us who stand so much in need of them.—*In Tune with the Infinite*

How Mind Builds Body

Would you remain always young, and would you carry all the joyousness and buoyancy of youth into your maturer years? Then have care concerning but one thing, — how you live in your thought world. This will determine all. It was the inspired one, Gautama, the Buddha, who said, — "The mind is everything; what you think you become." And the same thing had Ruskin in mind when he said, — "Make yourself nests of pleasant thoughts. None of us as yet know, for none of us have been taught in early youth, what fairy palaces we may build of beautiful thought, —proof against all adversity."

And would you have in your body all the elasticity, all the strength, all the beauty of your younger years? Then live these in your mind, making no room for unclean thought, and you will externalize them in your body. In the degree that you keep young in thought will you remain young in body. And you will find that your body will in turn aid your mind, for body helps mind the same as mind builds body.

You are continually building, and so externalizing in your body conditions most akin to the thoughts and emotions you entertain. And not only are you so building from within, but you are also continually drawing from without, forces of a kindred nature. Your particular kind of thought connects you with a similar order of thought from without. If it is bright, hopeful, cheerful, you connect yourself with a current of thought of this nature. If it is sad, fearing, despondent, then this is the order of thought you connect yourself with.

If the latter is the order of your thought, then perhaps unconsciously and by degrees you have been connecting yourself with it. You need to go back and pick up again a part of your child nature, with its careless and cheerful type of thought.

Full, rich, and abounding health is the normal and the natural condition of life. Anything else is an abnormal condition, and abnormal conditions as a rule come through perversions. God never created sickness, suffering, and disease; they are man's own creations. They come through his violating the laws under which he lives. So used are we to seeing them that we come gradually, if not to think of them as natural, then to look upon them as a matter of course.

The time will come when the work of the physician will not be to treat and attempt to heal the body, but to heal the mind, which in turn will heal the body. In other words, the true physician will be a teacher; his work will be to keep people well, instead of attempting to make them well after sickness and disease comes on; and still beyond this there will come a time when each will be his own physician. In the degree that we live in harmony with the higher laws of our being, and so, in the degree that we become better acquainted with the powers of the mind and spirit, will we give less attention to the body, — no less care, but less attention.

The bodies of thousands today would be much better cared for if their owners gave them less thought and attention. As a rule, those who think least of their bodies enjoy the best health. Many are kept in continual ill health by the abnormal thought and attention they give them.

Give the body the nourishment, the exercise, the fresh air, the sunlight it requires, keep it clean, and then think of it as little as possible. In your thoughts and in your conversation never dwell upon the negative side. Don't talk of sickness and disease. By talking of these you do yourself harm and you do harm to those who listen to you. Talk of those things that will make people the better for listening to you. Thus you will infect them with health and strength and not with weakness and disease. "Never affirm or repeat about your health what you do not wish to be true. Do not dwell upon your ailments, nor study your symptoms. Never allow yourself to be convinced that you are not complete master of yourself.

Stoutly affirm your superiority over bodily ills, and do not acknowledge yourself the slave of any inferior power. . . . I would teach children early to build a strong barrier between themselves and disease, by healthy habits of thought, high thinking, and purity of life. I would teach them to expel all thoughts of death, all images of disease, all discordant emotions, like hatred, malice, revenge, envy, and sensuality, as they would banish a temptation to do evil. I would teach them that bad food, bad drink, or bad air makes bad blood; that bad blood makes bad tissue, and bad flesh bad morals. I would teach them that healthy thoughts are as essential to healthy bodies as pure thoughts to a clean life. I would teach them to cultivate a strong will power, and to brace themselves against life's enemies in every possible way. I would teach the sick to have hope, confidence, cheer. Our thoughts and imaginations are the only real limits to our possibilities. No man's success or health will ever reach beyond his own confidence; as a rule, we erect our own barriers."—*In Tune with the Infinite*

Soul Radiance

All the frictions, all the uncertainties, all the ills, the sufferings, the fears, the forebodings, the perplexities of life come to us because we are out of harmony with the divine order of things. They will continue to come as long as we so live. Rowing against the tide is hard and uncertain. To go with the tide and thus to take advantage of the working of a great natural force is safe and easy. To come into the conscious, vital realization of our oneness with the Infinite Life and Power is to come into the current of this divine sequence. Coming thus into harmony with the Infinite, brings us in turn into harmony with all about us, into harmony with the life of the heavens, into harmony with all the universe. And above all, it brings us into harmony with ourselves, so that body, soul, and mind become perfectly harmonized, and when this is so, life becomes full and complete.

The sense life then no longer masters and enslaves us. The physical is subordinated to and ruled by the mental; this in turn is subordinated to and continually illumined by the spiritual. Life is then no longer the poor, one-sided thing it is in so many cases; but the three-fold, the all-round life with all its beauties and ever increasing joys and powers is entered upon. Thus it is that we are brought to realize that the middle path is the great solution of life; neither asceticism on the one hand nor license and perverted use on the other. Everything is for use, but all must be wisely used in order to be fully enjoyed.

As we live in these higher realizations the senses are not ignored but are ever more fully perfected. As the body becomes less gross and heavy, finer in its texture and form, all the senses become finer, so that powers we do not now realize as belonging to us gradually develop. Thus we come, in a perfectly natural and normal way, into the super-conscious realms whereby we make it possible for the higher laws and truths to be revealed to us. As we enter into these realms we are then not among those who give their time to speculating as to whether this one or that one had the insight and the powers attributed to him, but we are able to know for ourselves. Neither are we among those who attempt to lead the people upon the hearsay of someone else, but we know whereof we speak, and only thus can we speak with authority.

There are many things that we cannot know until by living the life we bring ourselves into that state where it is possible for them to be revealed to us. "If any man will do His will, he shall know of the doctrine." It was Plotinus who said, "The mind that wishes to behold God must itself become God." As we thus make it possible for these higher laws and truths to be revealed to us, we will in turn become enlightened ones, channels through which they may be revealed to others.

When one is fully alive to the possibilities that come with this higher awakening, as he goes here and there, as he mingles with his fellow-men, he imparts to all an inspiration that kindles in them a feeling of power kindred to his own. We are all continually giving out influences similar to those that are playing in our own lives. We do this in the same way that each flower emits its own peculiar odor. The rose breathes out its fragrance upon the air and all who come near it are refreshed and inspired by this emanation from the soul of the rose.

A poisonous weed sends out its obnoxious odor; it is neither refreshing nor inspiring in its effects, and if one remain near it long he may be so unpleasantly affected as to be made even ill by it. The higher the life the more inspiring and helpful are the emanations that it is continually sending out. The lower the life the more harmful is the influence it continually sends out to all who come in contact with it. Each one is continually radiating an atmosphere of one kind or the other.

We are told by the mariners who sail on the Indian Seas, that many times they are able to tell their approach to certain islands long before they can see them by the sweet fragrance of the sandalwood that is wafted far out upon the deep. Do you not see how it would serve to have such a soul playing through such a body that as you go here and there a subtle, silent force goes out from you that all feel and are influenced by; so that you carry with you an inspiration and continually shed a benediction wherever you go; so that your friends and all people will say, — His coming brings peace and joy into our homes, welcome his coming; so that as you pass along the street, tired, and weary, and even sinsick men and women will feel a certain divine touch that will awaken new desires and a new life in them; that will make the very horse as you pass him turn his head with a strange, half-human, longing look? Such are the subtle powers of the human soul when it makes itself translucent to the Divine.—*In Tune with the Infinite*

Intuition: The Voice Of The Soul

The power of every life, the very life itself, is determined by what it relates itself to. God is immanent as well as transcendent. He is creating, working, ruling in the universe today, in your life and in mine, just as much as He ever has been. We are too apt to regard Him after the manner of an absentee landlord, one who has set in operation the forces of this great universe, and then taken Himself away.

In the degree, however, that we recognize Him as immanent as well as transcendent, are we able to partake of His life and power. For in the degree that we recognize Him as the Infinite Spirit of Life and Power that is today, at this very moment, working and manifesting in and through all, and then, in the degree that we come into the realization of our oneness with this life, do we become partakers of, and so do we actualize in ourselves the qualities of His life. In the degree that we open ourselves to the inflowing tide of this immanent and transcendent life, do we make ourselves channels through which the Infinite Intelligence and Power can work.

It is through the instrumentality of the mind that we are enabled to connect the real soul life with the physical life, and so enable the soul life to manifest and work through the physical. The thought life needs continually to be illumined from within. This illumination can come in just the degree that through the agency of the mind we recognize our oneness with the Divine, of which each soul is an individual form of expression.

This gives us the inner guiding which we call intuition. "Intuition is to the spiritual nature and understanding practically what sense perception is to the sensuous nature and understanding. It is an inner spiritual sense through which man is opened to the direct revelation and knowledge of God, the secrets of nature and life, and through which he is brought into conscious unity and fellowship with God, and made to realize his own deific nature and supremacy of being as the son of God.... It is, we repeat, a spiritual sense opening inwardly, as the physical senses open outwardly; and because it has the capacity to perceive, grasp, and know the truth at first hand, independent of all external sources of information, we call it intuition. All inspired teaching and spiritual revelations are based upon the recognition of this spiritual faculty of the soul, and its power to receive and appropriate them"

Some call it the voice of the soul; some call it the voice of God; some call it the sixth sense. It is our inner spiritual sense. In the degree that we come into the recognition of our own true selves, into the realization of the oneness of our life with the Infinite Life, and in the degree that we open ourselves to this divine inflow, does this voice of intuition, this voice of the soul, this voice of God, speak clearly; and in the degree that we recognize, listen to, and obey it, does it speak ever more clearly, until by-and-by there comes the time when it is unerring, absolutely unerring, in its guidance.—*In Tune with the Infinite*

Miracles And The Higher Life

The most powerful agent in character-building is this awakening to the true self, to the fact that man is a spiritual being — nay, more, that I, this very eternal I, am a spiritual being, right here and now, at this very moment, with the God-powers which can be quickly called forth. With this awakening, life in all its manifold relations becomes wonderfully simplified, And as to the powers, the full realization of the fact that man is a spiritual being and a living as such brings, they are absolutely without limit, increasing in direct proportion as the higher self, the God-self, assumes the mastery, and so as this higher spiritualization of life goes on.

With this awakening and realization one is brought at once en rapport with the universe. He feels the power and the thrill of the life universal. He goes out from his own little garden spot, and mingles with the great universe; and the little perplexities, trials, and difficulties of life that today so vex and annoy him, fall away of their own accord by reason of their very insignificance, The intuitions become keener and ever more keen and unerring in their guidance. There comes more and more the power of reading men, so that no harm can come from this source. There comes more and more the power of seeing into the future, so that more and more true becomes the old adage, — that coming events cast their shadows before.

Health in time takes the place of disease; for all disease and its consequent suffering is merely the result of the violation of law, either consciously or unconsciously, either intentionally or unintentionally. There comes also a spiritual power which, as it is sent out, is adequate for the healing of others the same as in the days of old. The body becomes less gross and heavy, finer in its texture and form, so that it serves far better and responds far more readily to the higher impulses of the soul. Matter itself in time responds to the action of these higher forces; and many things that we are accustomed by reason of our limited vision to call miraculous or supernatural become the normal, the natural, the everyday.

For what, let us ask, is a miracle? Nothing more nor less than this: a highly illumined soul, one who has brought his life into thorough harmony with the higher spiritual laws and forces of his being, and therefore with those of the universe, thus making it possible for the highest things to come to him, has brought to him a law a little higher than the ordinary mind knows of as yet. This he touches, he operates. It responds. The people see the result, and cry out, Miracle! miracle! when it is just as natural, just as fully in accordance with the law on this higher plane, as is the common, the everyday on the ordinary. And let it be remembered that the miraculous, the supernatural of today becomes, as in the process of evolution we leave the lower for the higher, the common-place, the natural, the everyday of tomorrow; and, truly, miracles are being performed in the world today just as much as they ever have been.

The Master never claimed for Himself anything that he did not claim for all mankind; but, quite to the contrary, He said and continually repeated, "Not only shall ye do these things, but greater than these shall ye do; for I have pointed out to you the way," — meaning, though strange as it evidently seems to many, exactly what He said.—*In Tune with the Infinite*

The Voice Of The Higher Self

Great should be the joy that God's boundless truth is open to all, open equally to all, and that it will make each one its dwelling place in proportion as he earnestly desires it and opens himself to it.

And in regard to the wisdom that guides us in our daily life, there is nothing that it is right and well for us to know that may not be known when we recognize the law of its coming, and are able wisely to use it. Let us know that all things are ours as soon as we know how to appropriate them.

"I hold it as a changeless law, from which no soul can sway or swerve, we have that in us which will draw whate'er we need or most deserve."

If the times come when we know not what course to pursue, when we know not which way to turn, the fault lies in ourselves. If the fault lies in ourselves then the correction of this unnatural condition lies also in ourselves. It is never necessary to come into such a state if we are awake and remain awake to the light and the powers within us. The light is ever shining, and the only thing that it is necessary for us diligently to see to is that we permit neither this thing nor that to come between us and the light. "With Thee is the fountain of life; in Thy light shall we see light."

Let us hear the words of one of the most highly illumined men I have ever known, and one who as a consequence is never in the dark, when the time comes, as to what to do and how to do it. " Whenever you are in doubt as to the course you should pursue, after you have turned to every outward means of guidance, let the inward eye see, let the inward ear hear, and allow this simple, natural, beautiful process to go on unimpeded by questionings or doubts.... In all dark hours and times of unwanted perplexity we need to follow one simple direction, found, as all needed directions can be found, in the dear old gospel, which so many read, but alas, so few interpret. 'Enter into thine inner chamber and shut the door.' Does this mean that we must literally betake ourselves to a private closet with a key in the door? If it did, then the command could never be obeyed in the open air, on land or sea, and the

Christ loved the lakes and the forests far better than the cramping rooms of city dwelling houses; still His counsels are so wide-reaching that there is no spot on earth and no conceivable situation in which any of us may be placed where we cannot follow them.

"One of the most intuitive men we ever met had a desk in a city office where several other gentlemen were doing business constantly and often talking loudly. Entirely undisturbed by the many various sounds about him, this self-centred, faithful man would, in any moment of perplexity, draw the curtains of privacy so completely about him that he would be as fully enclosed in his own psychic aura, and thereby as effectually removed from all distractions as though he were alone in some primeval wood. Taking his difficulty with him into the mystic silence in the form of a direct question, to which he expected a certain answer, he would remain utterly passive until the reply came, and never once through many years' experience did he find himself disappointed or misled. Intuitive perceptions of truth are the daily bread to satisfy our daily hunger; they come like the manna in the desert day by day; each day brings adequate supply for that day's need only. They must be followed instantly, for dalliance with them means their obscuration.

"One condition is imposed by universal law, and this we must obey. Put all wishes aside save the one desire to know truth; couple with this one demand — the fully consecrated determination to follow what is distinctly perceived as truth immediately it is revealed. No other affection must be permitted to share the field with this all-absorbing love of truth for its own sake. Obey this one direction and never forget that expectation and desire are bride and bridegroom and forever inseparable, and you will soon find your hitherto darkened way grow luminous with celestial radiance, for with the heaven within, all heavens without incessantly cooperate."

This may be termed going into the "silence." This it is to perceive and to be guided by "the light that lighteth every man that cometh into the world." This it is to listen to and be guided by the voice of your own soul, the voice of your higher self.—*In Tune with the Infinite*

The Soul Must Be Made
Translucent To The Divine

The soul is divine and in allowing it to become translucent to the Infinite Spirit it reveals all things to us. As man turns away from the Divine Light do all things become hidden. There is nothing hidden of itself. When the spiritual sense is opened, then it transcends all the limitations of the physical senses and the intellect. And in the degree that we are able to get away from the limitations set by them, and realize that so far as the real life is concerned it is one with the Infinite Life, then we begin to reach the place where this voice will always speak, where it will never fail us, if we follow it, and as a consequence where we will always have the divine illumination and guidance. To know this and to live in this realization is not to live in heaven hereafter, but to live in heaven here and now, today and everyday.

No human soul need be without it. When we turn our face in the right direction it comes as simply and as naturally as the flower blooms and the winds blow. It is not to be bought with money or with price. It is a condition waiting simply to be realized, by rich and by poor, by king and by peasant, by master and by servant the world over. All are equal heirs to it. And so the peasant, if he find it first, lives a life far transcending in beauty and in real power the life of his king. The servant, if he find it first, lives a life surpassing the life of his master.

If you would find the highest, the fullest, and the richest life that not only this world but that any world can know, then do away with the sense of the separateness of your life from the life of God. Hold to the thought of your oneness. In the degree that you do this you will find yourself realizing it more and more, and as this life of realization is lived, you will find that no good thing will be withheld, for all things are included in this. Then it will be yours, without fears or forebodings, simply to do today what your hands find to do, and so be ready for tomorrow, when it comes, knowing that tomorrow will bring tomorrow's supplies for the mental, the spiritual, and the physical life. Remember, however, that tomorrow's supplies are not needed until tomorrow comes.

If one is willing to trust himself fully to the Law, the Law will never fail him. It is the half-hearted trusting to it that brings uncertain, and so, unsatisfactory results. Nothing is firmer and surer than Deity. It will never fail the one who throws himself wholly upon it. The secret of life then, is to live continually in this realization, whatever one may be doing, wherever one may be, by day and by night, both waking and sleeping. It can be lived in while we are sleeping no less than when we are awake.—*In Tune with the Infinite*

Receiving Instruction During Sleep

During the process of sleep it is merely the physical body that is at rest and in quiet; the soul life with all its activities goes right on. Sleep is nature's provision for the recuperation of the body, for the rebuilding and hence the replacing of the waste that is continually going on during the waking hours. It is nature's great restorer. If sufficient sleep is not allowed the body, so that the rebuilding may equalize the wasting process, the body is gradually depleted and weakened, and any ailment or malady, when it is in this condition, is able to find a more ready entrance. It is for this reason that those who are subject to it will take a cold, as we term it, more readily when the body is tired or exhausted through loss of sleep than at most any other time. The body is in that condition where outside influences can have a more ready effect upon it, than when it is in its normal condition. And when they do have an effect they always go to the weaker portions first.

Our bodies are given us to serve far higher purposes than we ordinarily use them for. Especially is this true in the numerous cases where the body is master of its owner. In the degree that we come into the realization of the higher powers of the mind and spirit, in that degree does the body, through their influence upon it, become less gross and heavy, finer in its texture and form. And then, because the mind finds a kingdom of enjoyment in itself, and in all the higher things it becomes related to, excesses in eating and drinking, as well as all others, naturally and of their own accord fall away. There also falls away the desire for the heavier, grosser, less valuable kinds of food and drink, such as the flesh of animals, alcoholic drinks, and all things of the class that stimulate the body and the passions rather than build the body and the brain into a strong, clean, well-nourished, enduring, and fibrous condition.

In the degree that the body thus becomes less gross and heavy, finer in its texture and form, is there less waste, and what there is is more easily replaced, so that it keeps in a more regular and even condition. When this is true, less sleep is actually required. And even the amount that is taken does more for a body of this finer type than it can do for one of the other nature. As the body in this way grows finer, in other words, as the process of its evolution is thus accelerated, it in turn helps the mind and the soul in the realization of ever higher perceptions, and thus body helps mind the same as mind builds body. It was undoubtedly this fact that Browning had in mind when he said: "Let us cry: All good things are ours, nor soul helps flesh, more now, than flesh helps soul."

Sleep, then, is for the resting and the rebuilding of the body. The soul needs no rest, and while the body is at rest in sleep the soul life is active the same as when the body is in activity. There are some, having a deep insight into the soul's activities, who say that we travel when we sleep. Some are able to recall and bring over into the conscious, waking life the scenes visited, the information gained, and the events that have transpired. Most people are not able to do this and so much that might otherwise be gained is lost. They say, however, that it is in our power, in proportion as we understand the laws, to go where we will, and to bring over into the conscious, waking life all the experiences thus gained. Be this, however, as it may, it certainly is true that while sleeping we have the power, in a perfectly normal and natural way, to get much of value by way of light, instruction, and growth that the majority of people now miss.

If the soul life, that which relates us to Infinite Spirit, is always active, even while the body is at rest, why may not the mind so direct conditions as one falls asleep, that while the body is at rest, it may continually receive illumination from the soul and bring what it thus receives over into the conscious, waking life? This, indeed, can be done, and is done by some to great advantage; and many times the highest inspirations from the soul come in this way, as would seem most natural, since at this time all communications from the outer, material world no longer enter. By charging the mind on going to sleep as to a particular time for waking, it is possible as many of us know, to wake on the very minute. The mind acting intently along a particular line will continue so to act until some other object of thought carries it along another line. And since in sleep only the body is in quiet while the mind and soul are active, then the mind on being given a certain direction when one drops off to sleep, will take up the line along which it is directed, and can be made, in time, to bring over into consciousness the results of its activities. Some will be able very soon to get results of this kind; for some it will take longer. Quiet and continued effort will increase the faculty.—*In Tune with the Infinite*

The Joseph Type Both
Dreams And Interprets

Then by virtue of the law of the drawing power of mind, since the mind is always active, we are drawing to us even while sleeping, influences from the realms kindred to those in which we in our thoughts are living before we fall asleep. In this way we can put ourselves into relation with whatever kinds of influence we choose and accordingly gain much during the process of sleep. In many ways the interior faculties are more open and receptive while we are in sleep than while we are awake. Hence the necessity of exercising even greater care as to the nature of the thoughts that occupy the mind as we enter into sleep, for there can come to us only what we by our own order of thought attract. We have it entirely in our own hands.

And for the same reason, — this greater degree of receptivity during this period, — we are able by understanding and using the law, to gain much of value more readily in this way than when the physical senses are fully open to the material world about us. Many will find a practice somewhat after the following nature of value: When light or information is desired along any particular line, light or information you feel it is right and wise for you to have, as, for example, light in regard to an uncertain course of action, then as you retire, first bring your mind into the attitude of peace and good-will for all. You in this way bring yourself into an harmonious condition, and in turn attract to yourself these same peaceful conditions from without.

Then resting in this sense of peace, quietly and calmly send out your earnest desire for the needed light or information; cast out of your mind all fears or forebodings lest it come not, for "in quietness and in confidence shall be your strength." Take the expectant attitude of mind, firmly believing and expecting that when you awake the desired results will be with you. Then on awaking, before any thoughts or activities from the outside world come in to absorb the attention, remain for a little while receptive to the intuitions or the impressions that come. When they come, when they manifest themselves clearly, then act upon them without delay. In the degree that you do this, in that degree will the power of doing it ever more effectively grow.

Or, if for unselfish purposes you desire to grow and develop any of your faculties, or to increase the health and strength of your body, take a corresponding attitude of mind, the form of which will readily suggest itself in accordance with your particular needs or desires. In this way you will open yourself to, you will connect yourself with, and you will set into operation within yourself, the particular order of forces that will make for these results. Don't be afraid to voice your desires. In this way you set into operation vibratory forces which go out and which make their impress felt somewhere, and which, arousing into activity or uniting with other forces, set about to actualize your desires. No good thing shalt be withheld from him who lives in harmony with the higher laws and forces. There are no desires that shall not be satisfied to the one who knows and who wisely uses the powers with which he or she is endowed.

Your sleep will be more quiet, and peaceful, and refreshing, and so your power increased mentally, physically, and spiritually, simply by sending out as you fall asleep, thoughts of love and good-will, thoughts of peace and harmony for all. In this way you are connecting yourself with all the forces in the universe that make for peace and harmony.

Visions and inspirations of the highest order will come in the degree that we make for them the right conditions. One who has studied deeply into the subject in hand has said: "To receive education spiritually while the body is resting in sleep is a perfectly normal and orderly experience, and would occur definitely and satisfactorily in the lives of all of us, if we paid more attention to internal and consequently less to external states with their supposed but unreal necessities... Our thoughts make us what we are here and hereafter, and our thoughts are often busier by night than by day, for when we are asleep to the exterior we can be wide awake to the interior world; and the unseen world is a substantial place, the conditions of which are entirely regulated by mental and moral attainments.

"When we are not deriving information through outward avenues of sensation, we are receiving instruction through interior channels of perception, and when this fact is understood for what it is worth, it will become a universal custom for persons to take to sleep with them the special subject on which they most earnestly desire particular instruction. The Pharaoh type of person dreams, and so does his butler and baker; but the Joseph type, which is that of the truly gifted seer, both dreams and interprets."—*In Tune with the Infinite*

Humaneness In Our Diet

" Is not flesh-eating natural?" I hear it asked. "Does not man in his primitive, savage state make use of flesh naturally? Do not animals devour one another?" Yes; but we are not savages, nor are we purely animals, and it is time for us to have outgrown this attendant-of-savage-life custom. The truth of the matter is that considerably more than one-half of the people in the world today are not flesh-eaters. And many peoples, whom large numbers in America and England, for example, refer to as the heathen, and send missionaries to Christianize, are far ahead of us, and hence more Christian in this matter.

And one reason why missionaries in many parts of India, among the Buddhists and Brahmins, for example. have been so comparatively unsuccessful in their work is because the majority of those keen-minded and spiritually unfolded people cannot see what superiority there is in the religion of the one whom it allows to kill, cook, and feast upon the bodies of his or her fellow-creatures, which they themselves could not do.

In Bombay, to have the carcasses of animals exposed to public view, as we see them in the stores and markets here, and at times scores of them decorating the windows and entire fronts, is prohibited by law.

No, experience will teach you that if you do away with flesh-eating and get in its place the other valuable foods, the time will quickly come when you will care less and less for it; then again, the time will come when you will have no desire for it, and finally, you will grow positively to dislike it and its effects, and nothing could induce you to return again to the flesh-pots. And as for those who think that the ones who are not flesh-eaters are necessarily weaklings, I should like to match a friend of mine, an instructor in one of our great American universities, who for over eighteen years has eaten no flesh foods, — I should like to match him with any whom they may send forward, when it comes to a test of long continued work and endurance.

In London there are already numbers of restaurants where no flesh foods are served; in Berlin there are already about twenty, and their number in these, as well as in numerous other cities, is continually increasing. It is a matter of but a short time until there will be numbers of such in our own country. The only really consistent humanitarian is the one who is not a flesh-eater; and great, I am satisfied, will be the results, both to the human family and to the animal race, as children are wisely taught and judiciously directed along this line.

When one goes into the better restaurants where no flesh foods are served, in England and Germany for example, one is impressed with the foundationless excuse of so many people that it is hard, or even impossible, to get along without flesh foods. In the vegetable realm will be found an abundance, a hundred or a thousand times over, and especially when we begin to give some little attention to the great varieties of most valuable foods there, and to the exceedingly appetising ways in which they can be prepared. One reason why such large numbers of people feel that meat is a necessity, or almost a necessity with them as an article of food, is because in our hotels and restaurants and cafes, and, in fact, in the majority of our homes, the meat element forms the chief portion of the foods prepared for our tables, and to it, practically, all the skill in preparation is given; while the other things are looked upon more as accessories, and are many times prepared in an exceedingly careless manner, much as mere accessories would be. But with a decreasing use of flesh foods and with more attention given to the skilful preparation of the large numbers of other still more valuable foods, we shall begin to wonder why we have so long been slaves to a mere custom, thinking it a necessity.

The time will come in the world's history, and a movement is setting in that direction even now, when it will be deemed as strange a thing to find a man or a woman who eats flesh as food, as it is now to find a man or a woman who refrains from eating it. And personally, I share the belief with many others, that the highest mental, physical, and spiritual excellence will come to a person only when, among other things, he refrains from a flesh and blood diet.

And there is another matter of grave importance that we should not be allowed to lose sight of in this connection. The brutality to the animal creation, which as a weaker creation we should protect and care for, has its corresponding and balancing element in connection with our duty to those who are hired to do our butchery for us.

Each one who aids in creating the demand for flesh foods is to a greater or less extent, not indirectly but directly, responsible for the degrading and dehumanizing influences at work in the lives of many thousands of their fellow-men. We are our brother's keeper whenever it comes to a matter that we are personally involved in, and there are responsibilities that we cannot shift after we are once made acquainted with the facts pertaining to them.—*Every Living Creature*

To Be At Peace

A deep interior meaning underlies the great truth, "To be spiritually minded is life and peace." To recognize the fact that we are spirit, and to live in this thought, is to be spiritually minded, and so to be in harmony and peace. Oh, the thousands of men and women all about us weary with care, troubled and ill at ease, running hither and thither to find peace, weary in body, soul, and mind; going to other countries, traveling the world over, coming back, and still not finding it. Of course they have not found it and they never will find it in this way, because they are looking for it where it is not. They are looking for it without when they should look within. Peace is to be found only within, and unless one find it there he will never find it at all.

Peace lies not in the external world. It lies within one's own soul. We may travel over many different avenues in pursuit of it, we may seek it through the channels of the bodily appetites and passions, we may seek it through all the channels of the external, we may chase for it hither and thither, but it will always be just beyond our grasp, because we are searching for it where it is not. In the degree, however, that we order the bodily appetites and passions in accordance with the promptings of the soul within will the higher forms of happiness and peace enter our lives; but in the degree that we fail in doing this will disease, suffering, and discontent enter in.

To be at one with God is to be at peace. The child simplicity is the greatest agency in bringing this full and complete realization, the child simplicity that recognizes its true relations with the Father's life. There are people I know who have come into such a conscious realization of their oneness with this Infinite Life, this Spirit of Infinite Peace, that their lives are fairly bubbling over with joy. I have particularly in mind at this moment a comparatively young man who was an invalid for several years, his health completely broken with nervous exhaustion, who thought there was nothing in life worth living for, to whom everything and everybody presented a gloomy aspect and he in turn presented a gloomy aspect to all with whom he came in contact. Not long ago he came into such a vital realization of his oneness with this Infinite Power, he opened himself so completely to its divine inflow, that today he is in perfect health, and frequently as I meet him now he cannot resist the impulse to cry out, "Oh, it is a joy to be alive."

He who comes into this higher realization never has any fear, for he has always with him a sense of protection, and the very realization of this makes his protection complete. Of him it is true —"No weapon that is formed against thee shall prosper;" "There shall no ill come nigh thy dwelling;" " Thou shalt be in league with the stones of the field, and the beasts of the field shall be at peace with thee."

These are the men and the women who seem to live charmed lives. The moment we fear anything we open the door for the entrance of the actualization of the very thing we fear. An animal will never harm a person who is absolutely fearless in regard to it. The instant he fears he opens himself to danger; and some animals, the dog for example, can instantly detect the element of fear, and this gives him the courage to do harm. In the degree that we come into a full realization of our oneness with this Infinite Power do we become calm and quiet, undisturbed by the little occurrences that before so vex and annoy us. We are no longer disappointed in people, for we always read them aright. We have the power of penetrating into their very souls and seeing the underlying motives that are at work there.

As soon as we are able to read people aright we will then cease to be disappointed in them, we will cease to place them on pedestals, for this can never be done without some attendant disappointment. The fall will necessarily come, sooner or later, and moreover, we are thus many times unfair to our friends. When we come into harmony with this Spirit of Peace, evil reports and apparent bad treatment, either at the hands of friends or of enemies, will no longer disturb us. When we are conscious of the fact that in our life and our work we are true to that eternal principle of right, of truth, of justice that runs through all the universe, that unites and governs all, that always eventually prevails, then nothing of this kind can come nigh us, and come what may we will always be tranquil and undisturbed.

The things that cause sorrow, and pain, and bereavement will not be able to take the hold of us they now take, for true wisdom will enable us to see the proper place and know the right relations of all things. The loss of friends by the transition we call death will not cause sorrow to the soul that has come into this higher realization, for he knows that there is no such thing as death, for each one is not only a partaker, but an eternal partaker, of this Infinite Life. He knows that the mere falling away of the physical body by no means affects the real soul life. With a tranquil spirit born of a higher faith he can realize for himself, and to those less strong he can say:

"Loving friends! be wise and dry straightway every weeping eye; What you left upon the bier is not worth a single tear; 'Tis a simple sea-shell; one out of which the pearl has gone. The shell was nothing, leave it there; The pearl — the soul — was all, is here."

And so far as the element of separation is concerned, he realizes that to spirit there are no bounds, and that spiritual communion, whether between two persons in the body, or two persons, one in the body and one out of the body, is within the reach of all. In the degree that the higher spiritual life is realized can there be this higher spiritual communion.

In the degree that we are filled with this Spirit of Peace by thus opening ourselves to its inflow does it pour through us, so that we carry it with us wherever we go. In the degree that we thus open ourselves do we become magnets to attract peace from all sources; and in the degree that we attract and embody it in ourselves are we able to give it forth to others. We can in this way become such perfect embodiments of peace that wherever we go we are continually shedding benedictions.

There are people all around us who are continually giving out blessings and comfort, persons whose mere presence seems to change sorrow into joy, fear into courage, despair into hope, weakness into power. It is the one who has come into the realization of his own true self who carries this power with him and who radiates it wherever he goes — the one who, as we say, has found his center. And in all the great universe there is but one center — the Infinite Power that is working in and through all.—*In Tune with the Infinite*

Courage Begets Strength;
Fear Begets Weakness

The one who then has found his centre is the one who has come into the realization of his oneness with this Infinite Power, the one who recognizes himself as a spiritual being, for God is Spirit. Such is the man of power. Centred in the Infinite, he has thereby, so to speak, connected himself with, he has attached his belts to, the great power-house of the universe. He is constantly drawing power to himself from all sources. For, thus centred, knowing himself, conscious of his own power, the thoughts that go from his mind are thoughts of strength ;and by virtue of the law that like attracts like, he by his thoughts is continually attracting to himself from all quarters the aid of all whose thoughts are thoughts of strength, and in this way he is linking himself with this order of thought in the universe.

And so, "to him that hath, to him shall be given." This is simply the working of a natural law. His strong, positive, and hence constructive thought is continually working success for him along all lines, and continually bringing to him help from all directions. The things that he sees, that he creates in the ideal, are through the agency of this strong constructive thought continually clothing themselves, taking form, manifesting themselves in the material. Silent, unseen forces are at work which will sooner or later be made manifest in the visible.

Fear and all thoughts of failure never suggest themselves to such a man; or if they do, they are immediately sent out of his mind, and so he is not influenced by this order of thought from without. He does not attract it to him. He is in another current of thought. Consequently the weakening, failure-bringing thoughts of the fearing, the vacillating, the pessimistic about him, have no influence upon him. The one who is of the negative, fearing kind not only has his energies and his physical agents weakened, or even paralyzed through the influence of this kind of thought that is born within him, but he also in this way connects himself with this order of thought in the world about him.

And in the degree that he does this does he become a victim to the weak, fearing, negative minds all around him. Instead of growing in power, he increases in weakness. He is in the same order of thought with those of whom it is true —"and even that which they have shall be taken away from them." This again is simply the working of a natural law, the same as is its opposite. Fearing lest I lose even what I have I hide it away in a napkin. Very well. I must then pay the price of my "fearing lest I lose."

Thoughts of strength both build strength from within and attract it from without. Thoughts of weakness actualize weakness from within and attract it from without. Courage begets strength, fear begets weakness. And so courage begets success, fear begets failure. It is the man or the woman of faith, and hence of courage, who is the master of circumstances, and who makes his or her power felt in the world. It is the man or the woman who lacks faith and who as a consequence is weakened and crippled by fears and forebodings, who is the creature of all passing occurrences.

What one lives in his invisible, thought world, he is continually actualizing in his visible, material world. If he would have any conditions different in the latter he must make the necessary change in the former. A clear realization of this great fact would bring success to thousands of men and women who all about us are now in the depths of despair. It would bring health, abounding health and strength to thousands now diseased and suffering. It would bring peace and joy to thousands now unhappy and ill at ease.

And oh, the thousands all about us who are continually living in the slavery of fear. The spirits within that should be strong and powerful, are rendered weak and impotent. Their energies are crippled, their efforts are paralyzed. "Fear is everywhere — fear of want, fear of starvation, fear of public opinion, fear of private opinion, fear that what we own today may not be ours tomorrow, fear of sickness, fear of death. Fear has become with millions a fixed habit. The thought is everywhere. The thought is thrown upon us from every direction.... To live in continual dread, continual cringing, continual fear of anything, be it loss of love, loss of money, loss of position or situation, is to take the readiest means to lose what we fear we shall."

By fear nothing is to be gained, but on the contrary, everything is to be lost. "I know this is true," says one, "but I am given to fear; it's natural to me and I can't help it." Can't help it! In saying this you indicate one great reason of your fear by showing that you do not even know yourself as yet. You must know yourself in order to know your powers, and not until you know them can you use them wisely and fully. Don't say you can't help it. If you think you can't, the chances are that you can't. If you think you can, and act in accordance with this thought, then not only are the chances that you can, but if you act fully in accordance with it, that you can and that you will is an absolute certainty.

It was Virgil who in describing the crew which in his mind would win the race, said of them — "They can because they think they can." In other words, this very attitude of mind on their part will infuse a spiritual power into their bodies that will give them the strength and endurance which will enable them to win.

Then take the thought that you can; take it merely as a seed-thought, if need be, plant it in your consciousness, tend it, cultivate it, and it will gradually reach out and gather strength from all quarters. It will focus and make positive and active the spiritual force within you that is now scattered and of little avail. II will draw to itself force from without. It will draw to your aid the influence of other minds of its own nature, minds that are fearless, strong, courageous. You will thus draw to yourself and connect yourself with this order of thought. If earnest and faithful, the time will soon come when all fear will lose its hold; and instead of being an embodiment of weakness and a creature of circumstances, you will find yourself a tower of strength and a master of circumstances.—*In Tune with the Infinite*

"And What Is Mine Shall Know My Face"

We need more faith in everyday life — faith in the power that works for good, faith in the Infinite God, and hence faith in ourselves created in His image. And however things at times may seem to go, however dark at times appearances may be, the knowledge of the fact that "the Supreme Power has us in its charge as it has the suns and endless systems of worlds in space," will give us the supreme faith that all is well with us, the same as all is well with the world. "Thou wilt keep him in perfect peace whose mind is stayed on Thee."

There is nothing firmer, and safer, and surer than Deity. Then, as we recognize the fact that we have it in our own hands to open ourselves ever more fully to this Infinite Power, and call upon it to manifest itself in and through us, we will find in ourselves an ever increasing sense of power. For in this way we are working in conjunction with it, and it in turn is working in conjunction with us. We are then led into the full realization of the fact that all things work together for good to those that love the good. Then the fears and forebodings that have dominated us in the past will be transmuted into faith, and faith when rightly understood and rightly used is a force before which nothing can stand.

Materialism leads naturally to pessimism. And how could it do otherwise? A knowledge of the Spiritual Power working in and through us as well as in and through all things, a power that works for righteousness, leads to optimism. Pessimism leads to weakness. Optimism leads to power. The one who is centred in Deity is the one who not only outrides every storm, but who through the faith, and so, the conscious power that is in him, faces storm with the same calmness and serenity that he faces fair weather; for he knows well beforehand what the outcome will be. He knows that underneath are the everlasting arms. He it is who realizes the truth of the injunction, "Rest in the Lord, wait patiently for Him and He shall give thee thy heart's desire." All shall be given, simply given, to him who is ready to accept it. Can anything be clearer than this?

In the degree, then, that we work in conjunction with the Supreme Power do we need the less to concern ourselves about results. To live in the full realization of this fact and all that attends it brings peace, a full, rich, abiding peace — a peace that makes the present complete, and that, going on before, brings back the assurance that as our days, so shall our strength be. The one who is thus centred, even in the face of all the unrest and the turmoil about us, can realize and say:

"I stay my haste, I make delays, for what avails this eager pace? I stand amid eternal ways, and what is mine shall know my face. Asleep, awake, by night or day, the friends I seek are seeking me; No wind can drive my bark astray, nor change the tide of destiny.

"The waters know their own, and draw the brooks that spring in yonder height; So flows the good with equal law unto the soul of pure delight.

"The stars come nightly to the sky; the tidal wave unto the sea; Nor time, nor space, nor deep, nor high, can keep my own away from me."—*In Tune with the Infinite*

Heredity And Environment
Are We Bound By Them?

The true secret of power lies in keeping one's connection with the God who worketh all things. Whatever can't be done in the physical can be done in the spiritual. And in direct proportion as a man recognizes himself as spirit, and lives accordingly, is he able to transcend in power the man who recognizes himself merely as material. All the sacred literature of the world is teeming with examples of what we call miracles. They are not confined to any particular times or places. There is no age of miracles in distinction from any other period that may be an age of miracles. Whatever has been done in the world's history can be done again through the operation of the same laws and forces. These miracles were performed not by those who were more than men, but by those who through the recognition of their oneness with God became God-men, so that the higher forces and powers worked through them.

For what, let us ask, is a miracle? Is it something supernatural? Supernatural only in the sense of being above the natural, or rather, above that which is natural to man in his ordinary state. A miracle is nothing more nor less than this. One who has come into a knowledge of his true identity, of his oneness with the all-pervading Wisdom and Power, thus makes it possible for laws higher than the ordinary mind knows of to be revealed to him. These laws he makes use of; the people see the results, and by virtue of their own limitations, call them miracles and speak of the person who performs these apparently supernatural works as a supernatural being.

But they as supernatural beings could themselves perform these supernatural works if they would open themselves to the recognition of the same laws, and consequently to the realization of the same possibilities and powers. And let us also remember that the supernatural of yesterday becomes, as in the process of evolution we advance from the lower to the higher, from the more material to the more spiritual, the common and the natural of today, and what seems to be the supernatural of today becomes in the same way the natural of tomorrow, and so on through the ages.

Yes, it is the God-man who does the things that appear supernatural, the man who by virtue of his realization of the higher powers transcends the majority and so stands out among them. But any power that is possible to one human soul is possible to another. The same laws operate in every life. We can be men and women of power or we can be men and women of impotence. The moment one vitally grasps the fact that he can rise he will rise, and he can have absolutely no limitations other than the limitations he sets to himself. Cream always rises to the top. It rises simply because it is the nature of cream to rise.

We hear much said of "environment." We need to realize that environment should never be allowed to make the man, but that man should always, and always can, condition the environment. When we realize this we will find that many times it is not necessary to take ourselves out of any particular environment, because we may yet have a work to do there; but by the very force we carry with us we can so affect and change matters that we will have an entirely new set of conditions in an old environment.

The same is true in regard to "hereditary" traits and influences. We sometimes hear the question asked, "Can they be overcome?" Only the one who doesn't yet know himself can ask a question such as this. If we entertain and live in the belief that they cannot be overcome, then the chances are that they will always remain. The moment, however, that we come into a realization of our true selves, and so of the tremendous powers and forces within — the powers and forces of the mind and spirit — hereditary traits and influences that are harmful in nature will begin to lessen, and will disappear with a rapidity directly in proportion to the completeness of this realization.

"There is no thing we cannot overcome; Say not thy evil instinct is inherited, or that some trait inborn makes thy whole life forlorn, and calls down punishment that is not merited.

Back of thy parents and grandparents lies The Great Eternal Will!, that too is thine Inheritance, — strong, beautiful, divine, sure lever of success for one who tries.

Earth has no claim the soul cannot contest; Know thyself part of the Eternal Source; Naught can stand before thy spirit's force: The soul's Divine Inheritance is best."—*In Tune with the Infinite*

Preserving One's Individuality

Again there are many who are living far below their possibilities because they are continually handing over their individualities to others. Do you want to be a power in the world? Then be yourself. Don't class yourself, don't allow yourself to be classed among the second-hand, among the they-say people. Be true to the highest within your own soul and then allow yourself to be governed by no customs or conventionalities or arbitrary man-made rules that are not founded upon principle. Those things that are founded upon principle will be observed by the right-minded, the right-hearted man or woman, in any case.

Don't surrender your individuality, which is your greatest agent of power, to the customs and conventionalities that have gotten their life from the great mass of those who haven't enough force to preserve their individualities — those who in other words have given them over as ingredients to the "mush of concession" which one of our greatest writers has said characterizes our modern society. If you do surrender your individuality in this way, you simply aid in increasing the undesirable conditions; in payment for this you become a slave, and the chances are that in time you will be unable to hold even the respect of those whom you in this way try to please.

If you preserve your individuality then you become a master, and if wise and discreet, your influence and power will be an aid in bringing about a higher, a better, and a more healthy set of conditions in the world. All people, moreover, will think more of you, will honor you more highly for doing this than if you show your weakness by contributing yourself to the same "mush of concession" that so many of them are contributing themselves to. With all classes of people you will then have an influence. "A great style of hero draws equally all classes, all extremes of society to him, till we say the very dogs believe in him."

To be one's self is the only worthy, and by all means the only satisfactory, thing to be. "When we appeal to the Supreme and our life is governed by a principle, we are not governed either by fear of public opinion or loss of others' approbation, and we may be sure that the Supreme will sustain us. If in any way we try to live to suit others we never shall suit them, and the more we try the more unreasonable and exacting do they become. The government of your life is a matter that lies entirely between God and yourself, and when your life is swayed and influenced from any other source you are on the wrong path." When we find the kingdom within and become centred in the Infinite, then we become a law unto ourselves. When we become a law unto ourselves, then we are able to bring others to a knowledge of laws higher than they are governed or many times even enslaved by.

When we have found this centre, then that beautiful simplicity, at once the charm and the power of a truly great personality, enters into our lives. Then all striving for effect — that sure indicator of weakness and a lack of genuine power — is absent. This striving for effect that is so common is always an indicator of a lack of something. It brings to mind the man who rides behind a dock-tailed horse. Conscious of the fact that there is not enough in himself to attract attention, in common with a number of other weaklings, he adopts the brutal method of having his horse's tail sawed off, that its unnatural, odd appearance may attract from people the attention that he of himself is unable to secure.

But the one who strives for effect is always fooled more than he succeeds in fooling others. The man and the woman of true wisdom and insight can always see the causes that prompt, the motives that underlie the acts of all with whom he or she comes in contact. " He is great who is what he is from nature and who never reminds us of others."

The men and the women who are truly awake to the real powers within are the men and women who seem to be doing so little, yet who in reality are doing so much. They seem to be doing so little because they are working with higher agencies, and yet are doing so much because of this very fact. They do their work on the higher plane. They keep so completely their connection with the Infinite Power that It does the work for them and they are relieved of the responsibility. They are the careless people. They are careless because it is the Infinite Power that is working through them, and with this Infinite Power they are simply co-operating.—*In Tune with the Infinite*

Exclusiveness And Inclusiveness: What They Indicate

When we come fully to realize the great fact that all evil and error and sin with all their consequent sufferings come through ignorance, then wherever we see a manifestation of these in whatever form, if our hearts are right, we will have compassion — sympathy and compassion for the one in whom we see them. Compassion will then change itself into love, and love will manifest itself in kindly service. Such is the divine method. And so instead of aiding in trampling and keeping a weaker one down, we will hold him up until he can stand alone and become the master.

By example and not by precept. By living, not by preaching. By doing, not by professing. By living the life, not by dogmatizing as to how it should be lived. There is no contagion equal to the contagion of life. Whatever we sow, that shall we also reap, and each thing sown produces of its kind. We can kill not only by doing another bodily injury directly, but we can and we do kill by every antagonistic thought. Not only do we thus kill, but while we kill we suicide. Many a man has been made sick by having the ill thoughts of a number of people centred upon him; some have been actually killed. Put hatred into the world and we make it a literal hell. Put love into the world and heaven with all its beauties and glories becomes a reality.

Not to love is not to live, or it is to live a living death. The life that goes out in love to all is the life that is full, and rich, and continually expanding in beauty and in power. Such is the life that becomes ever more inclusive, and hence larger in its scope and influence. The larger the man and the woman, the more inclusive they are in their love and their friendships. The smaller the man and the woman, the more dwarfed and dwindling their natures, the more they pride themselves upon their "exclusiveness." Anyone —a fool or an idiot —can be exclusive. It comes easy. It takes and it signifies a large nature to be universal, to be inclusive. Only the man or the woman of a small, personal, self-centred, self-seeking nature is exclusive.

The man or the woman of a large, royal, unself-centered nature never is. The small nature is the one that continually strives for effect. The larger nature never does. The one goes here and there in order to gain recognition, in order to attach himself to the world. The other stays at home and draws the world to him. The one loves merely himself. The other loves all the world; but in his larger love for all the world he finds himself included.

Verily, then, the more one loves the nearer he approaches to God, for God is the Spirit of Infinite Love. And when we come into the realization of our oneness with this Infinite Spirit, then divine love so fills us that, enriching and enrapturing our own lives, from them it flows out to enrich the life of all the world.

In coming into the realization of our oneness with the Infinite Life, we are brought at once into right relations with our fellowmen. We are brought into harmony with the great law, that we find our own lives in losing them in the service of others. We are brought to a knowledge of the fact that all life is one, and so that we are all parts of the one great whole. We then realize that we can't do for another without at the same time doing for ourselves. We also realize that we cannot do harm to another without by that very act doing harm to ourselves.

We realize that the man who lives to himself alone lives a little, dwarfed, and stunted life, because he has no part in this larger life of humanity. But the one who in service loses his own life in this larger life, has his own life increased and enriched a thousand or a million fold, and every joy, every happiness, everything of value coming to each member of this greater whole comes as such to him, for he has a part in the life of each and all. And here let a word be said in regard to true service. Peter and John were one day going up to the temple, and as they were entering the gate they were met by a poor cripple who asked them for alms. Instead of giving him something to supply the day's needs and then leaving him in the same dependent condition for the morrow and the morrow, Peter did him a real service, and a real service for all mankind by saying: Silver and gold have I none, but such as I have I give unto thee. And then he made him whole.

He thus brought him into the condition where he could help himself. In other words, the greatest service we can do for another is to help him to help himself. To help him directly might be weakening, though not necessarily. It depends entirely upon circumstances. But to help one to help himself is never weakening, but always encouraging and strengthening, because it leads him to a larger and stronger life.—*In Tune with the Infinite*

The Nature Of Real Riches

The one who has come into the realization of the higher life no longer has a desire for the accumulation of enormous wealth, anymore than he has a desire for any other excess. In the degree that he comes into the recognition of the fact that he is wealthy within, external wealth becomes less important in his estimation. When he comes into the realization of the fact that there is a source within from which he can put forth a power to call to him and actualize in his hands at any time a sufficient supply for all his needs, he no longer burdens himself with vast material accumulations that require his constant care and attention, and thus take his time and his thought from the real things of life. In other words, he first finds the kingdom, and he realizes that when he has found this, all other things follow in full measure.

Wealth beyond a certain amount cannot be used, and when it cannot be used it then becomes a hindrance rather than an aid, a curse rather than a blessing. All about us are persons with lives now stunted and dwarfed who could make them rich and beautiful, filled with a perennial joy, if they would begin wisely to use that which they have spent the greater portion of their lives in accumulating. The man who accumulates during his entire life, and who leaves even all when he goes out for "benevolent purposes," comes far short of the ideal life. It is but a poor excuse of a life.

It is not especially commendable in me to give a pair of old, worn-out shoes that I shall never use again to another who is in need of shoes. But it is commendable, if indeed doing anything we ought to do can be spoken of as being commendable, it is commendable for me to give a good pair of strong shoes to the man who in the midst of a severe winter is practically shoeless, the man who is exerting every effort to earn an honest living and thereby take care of his family's needs. And if in giving the shoes I also give myself, he then has a double gift, and I a double blessing.

There is no wiser use that those who have great accumulations can make of them than wisely to put them into life, into character, day by day while they live. In this way their lives will be continually enriched and increased. The time will come when it will be regarded as a disgrace for a man to die and leave vast accumulations behind him.

Many a person is living in a palace today who in the real life is poorer than many a one who has not even a roof to cover him. A man may own and live in a palace, but the palace for him may be a poorhouse still.

Moth and rust are nature's wise provisions —God's methods —for disintegrating and scattering, in this way getting ready for use in new forms, that which is hoarded and consequently serving no use. There is also a great law continually operating whose effects are to dwarf and deaden the powers of true enjoyment, as well as all the higher faculties of the one who hoards.

Multitudes of people are continually keeping away from them higher and better things because they are forever clinging on to the old. If they would use and pass on the old, room would be made for new things to come. Hoarding always brings loss in one form or another. Using, wisely using, brings an ever renewing gain.

If the tree should as ignorantly and as greedily hold on to this year's leaves when they have served their purpose, where would be the full and beautiful new life that will be put forth in the spring? Gradual decay and finally death would be the result. If the tree is already dead, then it may perhaps be well enough for it to cling on to the old, for no new leaves will come. But as long as the life in the tree is active, it is necessary that it rid itself of the old ones, that room may be made for the new.

Opulence is the law of the universe, an abundant supply for every need if nothing is put in the way of its coming. The natural and the normal life for us is this — To have such a fullness of life and power by living so continually in the realization of our oneness with the Infinite Life and Power that we find ourselves in the constant possession of an abundant supply of all things needed.

Then not by hoarding but by wisely using and ridding ourselves of things as they come, an ever renewing supply will be ours, a supply far better adapted to present needs than the old could possibly be, In this way we not only come into possession of the richest treasures of the Infinite Good ourselves, but we also become open channels through which they can flow to others.—*In Tune with the Infinite*

A Method Of Attainment

A living insight into the fact of the essential unity of the human life with the Divine Life is the profoundest knowledge that man can attain to. This as a mere intellectual perception, however, as a mere dead theory, amounts to but little, if indeed to anything at all, so far as bearing fruit in everyday life is concerned. It is the vital, living realization of this great transcendent truth in the life of each one that makes it a mighty moving and moulding force in his life.

It is only through this living realization of the essential unity of our life with the Father's life that true blessedness, and even true peace and happiness, can be found. The sooner, then, that we come into it, and thus live the life of the spirit, the better, for neither will they come nor can they be found in any other way, There is, moreover, no time either in this form of life, or in any other form, that we can any more readily come into it, and thereby into all that follows. And when this fountain of Divine Life is once fully opened within us, it can never again be dried up, and we can rest assured that it will at all times uphold us in peace and bear us on safety. And however strange or unaccountable at times occurrences may appear, we can rest in a triumphant security, knowing that only good can come, for in God's life there is only good, and in God's life we are now living, and there we shall live forever.

There is a simple method which will aid us greatly in coming into the realization we have been considering. So simple is it that thousands and indeed millions have passed it by, looking, as is so generally our custom, for agencies of at least apparently greater power; we so frequently and so universally forget that the greatest things in life are the most simple.

The method is this: wherever you are, whatever doing, walking along the street or through the fields, at work of any kind, falling off to or awaking from sleep, setting about any undertaking, in doubt as to what course to pursue at any particular time, in brief, whatever it may be, carry with you this thought: It is the Father that workfth in me, my Father works and I work. This is the thought so continually used by Jesus, who came into the fullest realization of the oneness of his life with the God-life that anyone who has lived in the world thus far has come into, and it is given because it is so simple.

From it each can make his own formula. Jesus' term was "the Father." Many will likewise find themselves naturally using the same term and will find it becoming very precious to them. Others will find themselves using other terms for the same conception and thought: It is the Father that worketh in me, my Father works and I work. In other words, It is the Spirit of Infinite Life and Power that is back of all, working in and through all, the life and animating power of all — God — that worketh in me, and I do as I am directed and empowered by It.

In this way we open ourselves, and become consciously awake to the Infinite Life and Power that is ever waiting and ready to direct and work in our lives, if we will merely put ourselves into the attitude whereby It can work in them. In this way we open ourselves so that It can speak and manifest to and through us. This It is ever ready to do if we will but make for It the right conditions. By carrying with us this thought, by holding ourselves in this attitude of mind consciously for awhile, by repeating it even in so many words now and then at first, we will find it in time becoming our habitual thought, and will find ourselves living in it without the conscious effort that we have to make at first, and we will in time find ourselves almost unconsciously living in it continually.

Thus God as a living presence, as a guiding, animating power, becomes an actuality in our lives. The conscious presence of God in our lives, which is the essence, indeed the sum and substance of all religion, then becomes a reality, and all wisdom and all power will be given us as we are able to appropriate and use then wisely; if for merely selfish, personal ends, they will be withheld; if for the greatest aid and service for the world, we will find them continually increasing.

With this higher realization comes more and more the simple, child-like spirit. With Jesus we realize —Of myself I can do nothing, it is the Father within me that doeth His work. In ourselves we are and can do nothing; in God we can do all things. We never can be in the condition — in God — until through this higher realization God becomes a conscious, living reality in our lives.

Faithfulness to this simple method will bring about a complete change in great numbers of lives. Each one for himself can test its efficacy in a very short time. It is the highway upon which many will enter that will by easy stages take them into the realization of the highest life that can be attained to. To set one's face in the right direction, and then simply to travel on, will in time bring him into the realization of the highest life that can be even conceived of — it is the secret of all attainment.

(from: *The Greatest Thing Ever Known*)

A Sort Of Creed

To be observed today, or in part; to be changed tomorrow — or abandoned — if the light is better.

To Live to our highest in all things that pertain to us; To lend a hand as best we can to all others for this same end;

To aid in righting the wrongs that cross our path by pointing the wrong-doer to a better way, and thus aid him in becoming a power for good;

To remain in nature always sweet and simple and humble, and therefore strong; To open ourselves fully and to keep ourselves pure and clean as fit channels for the Divine Power to work through us; To turn toward and keep our faces always to the light; To do our own thinking, listening quietly to the opinions of others, and to be sufficiently men and women to act always upon our own convictions;

To do our duty as we see it, regardless of the opinions of others, seeming gain or loss, temporary blame or praise; To play the part of neither knave nor fool by attempting to judge another, but to give that same time to living more worthily ourselves;

To get up immediately when we stumble, face again to the light, and travel on without wasting even a moment in regret; To love all things and to stand in awe or fear of nothing save our own wrong-doing;

To recognize the good lying at the heart of all people, of all things, waiting for expression, all in its own good way and time; To love the fields and the wild flowers, the stars, the far-open sea, the soft, warm earth, and to live much with them alone, but to love struggling and weary men and women and every pulsing living creature better;

To strive always to do unto others as we would have them do unto us

In brief — to be honest, to be fearless, to be just, to be kind. This will make our part in life's great and as yet not fully understood play truly glorious, and we need then stand in fear of nothing — life nor death; for death is life.

Or, rather, it is the quick transition to life in another form; the putting off of the old coat and the putting on of a new; a passing not from light to darkness but from light to light, according as we have lived here; a taking up of life in another form just where we leave it off here; a part in life not to be shunned or dreaded or feared, but to be welcomed with a glad and ready smile when it comes in its own good way and time.

CPSIA information can be obtained at www.ICGtesting.com
Printed in the USA
LVOW12s0710260614

391812LV00004B/257/A